The Constitution of the United States

A LOOK AT THE FOURTH AMENDMENT

AGAINST UNREASONABLE SEARCHES AND SEIZURES

DOREEN GONZALES

MyReportLinks.com Books

an imprint of

Enslow Publishers, Inc.

Box 398, 40 Industrial Road
Berkeley Heights, NJ 07922
USA

MyReportLinks.com Books, an imprint of Enslow Publishers, Inc. MyReportLinks®
is a registered trademark of Enslow Publishers, Inc.

Library of Congress Cataloging-in-Publication Data

Gonzales, Doreen.
  A look at the Fourth Amendment : against unreasonable searches and seizures / Doreen Gonzales.
    p. cm.
  Includes bibliographical references and index.
  ISBN-13: 978-1-59845-062-0
  ISBN-10: 1-59845-062-X
  1. United States. Constitution. 4th Amendment. 2. Searches and seizures—United States. 3.
Criminal procedure—United States. I. Title.
  KF9630.G66 2007
  345.73'0522—dc22

                             2006024157

Printed in the United States of America

10 9 8 7 6 5 4 3 2 1

To Our Readers:
Through the purchase of this book, you and your library gain access to the Report Links that specifically
back up this book.
The Publisher will provide access to the Report Links that back up this book and will keep these Report
Links up to date on **www.myreportlinks.com** for five years from the book's first publication date.
We have done our best to make sure all Internet addresses in this book were active and appropriate when
we went to press. However, the author and the Publisher have no control over, and assume no liability
for, the material available on those Internet sites or on other Web sites they may link to.
The usage of the MyReportLinks.com Books Web site is subject to the terms and conditions stated on the
Usage Policy Statement on **www.myreportlinks.com**.
A password may be required to access the Report Links that back up this book. The password is found
on the bottom of page 4 of this book.
Any comments or suggestions can be sent by e-mail to comments@myreportlinks.com or to the address
on the back cover.

CONTENTS

MyReportLinks.com Books
Great Books, Great Links, Great for Research!

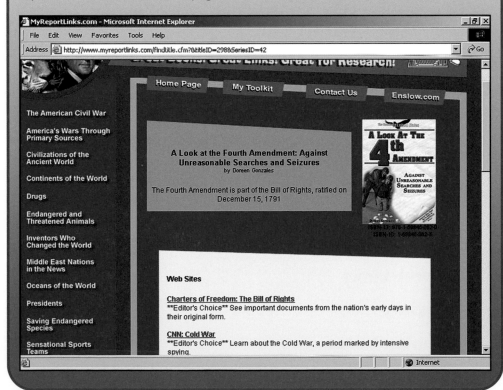

The Internet sites featured in this book can save you hours of research time. These Internet sites—we call them **"Report Links"**—are constantly changing, but we keep them up to date on our Web site.

When you see this "Approved Web Site" logo, you will know that we are directing you to a great Internet site that will help you with your research.

Give it a try! Type http://www.myreportlinks.com into your browser, click on the series title and enter the password, then click on the book title, and scroll down to the Report Links listed for this book.

The Report Links will bring you to great source documents, photographs, and illustrations. MyReportLinks.com Books save you time, feature Report Links that are kept up to date, and make report writing easier than ever! A complete listing of the Report Links can be found on pages 116–117 at the back of the book.

MyReportLinks.com - Microsoft Internet Explorer

File   Edit   View   Favorites   Tools   Help

Address http://www.myreportlinks.com/findtitle.cfm?&titleID=2988SeriesID=42

Home Page   My Toolkit   Contact Us   Enslow.com

The American Civil War

America's Wars Through Primary Sources

Civilizations of the Ancient World

Continents of the World

Drugs

Endangered and Threatened Animals

Inventors Who Changed the World

Middle East Nations in the News

Oceans of the World

Presidents

Saving Endangered Species

Sensational Sports Teams

A Look at the Fourth Amendment: Against Unreasonable Searches and Seizures
by Doreen Gonzales

The Fourth Amendment is part of the Bill of Rights, ratified on December 15, 1791

A LOOK AT THE 4th AMENDMENT

AGAINST UNREASONABLE SEARCHES AND SEIZURES

ISBN-13: 978-1-59845-062-0
ISBN-10: 1-59845-062-X

Web Sites

Charters of Freedom: The Bill of Rights
Editor's Choice See important documents from the nation's early days in their original form.

CNN: Cold War
Editor's Choice Learn about the Cold War, a period marked by intensive spying.

Internet

Please see "To Our Readers" on the copyright page for important information about this book, the MyReportLinks.com Web site, and the Report Links that back up this book.

Please enter **AFC1849** if asked for a password.

TIME LINE

1761 —Colonial lawyer James Otis appears before a Massachusetts court asking that it deny a writ of assistance. He loses the case.

1764 —Great Britain imposes the Sugar Act on the colonies. The Sugar Act taxes molasses. Colonists protest the new tax by smuggling.

1767 —The Townshend Acts place new taxes on the colonists. In addition to continued smuggling to avoid taxes, the colonists now refuse to buy British goods.

1770 —Using writs of assistance, the British raid homes, ships, warehouses, and stores
−1775 looking for smuggled goods, weapons, and documents about rebellion. The colonists fight back with protests and riots. In some cases they are able to shut down search operations.

—The American Revolutionary War begins in 1775.

1783 —The American Revolutionary War officially ends.

1791 —The Bill of Rights is added to the United States Constitution. It includes the Fourth Amendment.

1833 —In the case of *Barron* v. *Baltimore,* the Supreme Court rules that the Constitution protects people from the actions of the federal government. This means that the Fourth Amendment applies only to the actions of the federal government.

1914 —The Supreme Court rules in *Weeks* v. *U.S.* that evidence that is improperly seized cannot be used in a trial. This creates what is known as the Exclusionary Rule.

1925 —In *Carroll* v. *U.S.* the Court rules that cars can be searched without a warrant if there is probable cause.

1928 —The Supreme Court decides in *Olmstead* v. *U.S.* that government officials can wiretap homes and offices if there is no intrusion into a person's private space.

1949 —*Wolf* v. *Colorado* tests whether the Exclusionary Rule applies to states. The Supreme Court says it does not.

1961 —In *Mapp* v. *Ohio,* the Supreme Court overturns its 1949 decision by ruling that states do need to abide by the Exclusionary Rule.

1964 —The Supreme Court sets forth standards for probable cause in *Aguilar* v. *Texas.*

1967 —The Supreme Court overturns another earlier precedent. It decides in *Katz* v. *U.S.* that wiretappings and electronic eavesdroppings are in fact searches. Therefore, they need warrants. This ruling creates a principal called the expectation of privacy.

1968 —In *Terry* v. *Ohio,* the Court says that law officials who have a reasonable suspicion that someone is dangerous may stop and search that person without a warrant or probable cause.

1969 —The Court defines standards of probable cause when dealing with police informants in the case of *Spinelli* v. *U.S.*

—In *Chimel* v. *California,* the Court defines the physical area officers may search when arresting an individual.

TIME LINE (CONT.)

1971 —In *U.S.* v. *White,* the Supreme Court says that a law official may wear an eavesdropping device without a warrant or a suspect's knowledge.

1973 —The ruling in *Cupp* v. *Murphy* allows law officers to search without a warrant in the interest of protecting evidence.

1975 —The Church Committee Report reveals that some government agencies have
–1976   abused search and seizure principals.

1978 —Congress passes the Foreign Intelligence Surveillance Act (FISA). These laws tell how and when the government can search United States citizens it thinks are involved in activities that threaten national security.

1982 —In *Ross* v. *U.S.,* the Supreme Court restates its stand on car searches. It says that every part of a car and every container in a car may be searched without a warrant if an officer has probable cause.

1983 —In the case of *Illinois* v. *Gates,* the Court says that probable cause cannot be decided by a formula. It must be based on the totality of circumstances.

1984 —The Supreme Court creates the good faith principal in *U.S.* v. *Leon.* This idea says that if police have obtained a warrant and followed correct search procedures, any evidence they find can be used in court even if the warrant was improperly issued.

1985 —In *New Jersey* v. *T.L.O.,* the Court rules that students in public schools have a lower level of protection from the Fourth Amendment than the general public has.

1989 —The Court rules in *Florida* v. *Riley* that the Fourth Amendment does not protect objects seen from the air.

1989 —In *Skinner* v. *Railway Labor Executives Association,* the Supreme Court decides that warrantless and suspicionless drug testing of employees is allowed when the public's safety is at risk.

1990 —*Michigan State Police* v. *Sitz* establishes the government's right to conduct random drug testing of drivers.

1995 —The Supreme Court rules in *Vernonia School District* v. *Acton* that students in public school sports can be required to take drug tests.

2001 —The United States is attacked by a terrorist organization called al-Qaeda.

—The Congress passes the Patriot Act in an effort to help law enforcement agencies find terrorists and stop future attacks.

2005 —The United States public learns of an eavesdropping program by the NSA. Many people are disturbed by its failure to follow FISA laws.

2006 —Several groups file lawsuits questioning the legality of the NSA program. In addition, the public learns of another surveillance program that examines bank records of United States citizens suspected of having connections to terrorism. Questions about its legality begin to surface.

THE RIGHT TO PRIVACY

*I*n December 1974, *The New York Times* newspaper published an alarming article. It said that the United States government had been spying on American citizens. Almost immediately, the U.S. Congress formed a committee to investigate the charges. It was led by Senator Frank Church.

The committee reported its findings in 1975 and 1976. This report was often referred to as the Church Committee Report. Many things in it upset the public.

One finding described a government program involving Dr. Martin Luther King, Jr. The Federal Bureau of Investigation (FBI) had spent years spying on this respected civil rights leader.

→ THE CAMPAIGN AGAINST DR. KING

The FBI began tracking Dr. King in 1962. At first the FBI thought he might have ties to the Communist party. However, the agency found no evidence of this.[1]

Even so, it continued spying on King. It wiretapped his home and office. It even bugged his hotel rooms as he traveled across the United States. The FBI was looking

The Church Committee Report showed that the FBI had been spying on civil rights leader Dr. Martin Luther King, Jr. This photo of Dr. King was taken in 1964.

for information that would embarrass King. According to the report, the agency wanted to destroy the civil rights leader.[2]

During its investigations, committee members looked for reasons why the agency would want to ruin Dr. King. J. Edgar Hoover had been the FBI director at the time of the program. But now he was dead, so they could not question him. So committee members turned to other FBI officials for answers.

One FBI man told the committee that he felt the program against King was unjustified. King was not promoting criminal behavior, and he was not a danger to society.[3] The only reason for the program seemed to be Hoover's dislike for King. The Church Committee did find evidence of this.[4]

Hoover's distaste was deep. He even continued his attacks after Dr. King was assassinated in 1968. For example, in 1969, Hoover tried to prevent Congress from creating a national Martin Luther King Day. In 1970 he told reporters that King was the "last one in the world who should ever have received" the Nobel Peace Prize.[5] To many it seemed clear that Hoover had used his power as FBI director to harass King. This was illegal.

ILLEGAL SURVEILLANCE

Local, state, and federal law officials often investigate citizens. Sometimes this involves surveillance. A surveillance is a close watch. But most

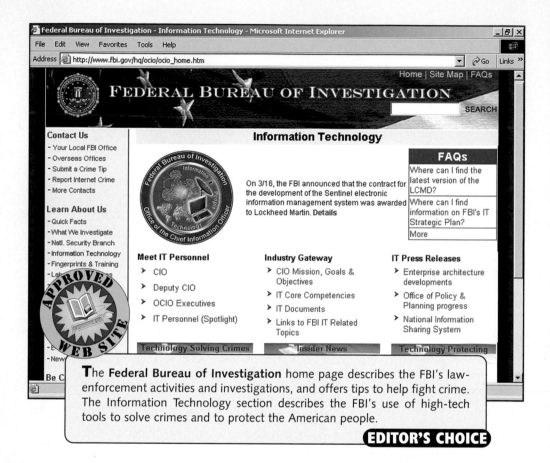

The **Federal Bureau of Investigation** home page describes the FBI's law-enforcement activities and investigations, and offers tips to help fight crime. The Information Technology section describes the FBI's use of high-tech tools to solve crimes and to protect the American people.

EDITOR'S CHOICE

kinds of government surveillance can only be done based on evidence that a crime has been committed. This includes listening in on telephone conversations and bugging personal spaces.

Furthermore, government officials cannot use electronic devices to spy on a person without permission from a judge. To do so without proper permission is a violation of the Fourth Amendment to the Constitution.

Hoover's surveillance of King was done without any suspicion of criminal activity. It was also done without permission from a judge. Both of these things made it against the law.

⊖THE PROGRAM TO CHECK MAIL

Martin Luther King, Jr., was not the only person who had been a victim of illegal government activities. The Church Committee Report revealed that during the 1960s and early 1970s, large numbers of law-abiding citizens had been the targets of illegal surveillance.

During these years, the FBI, the Central Intelligence Agency (CIA), and the National Security

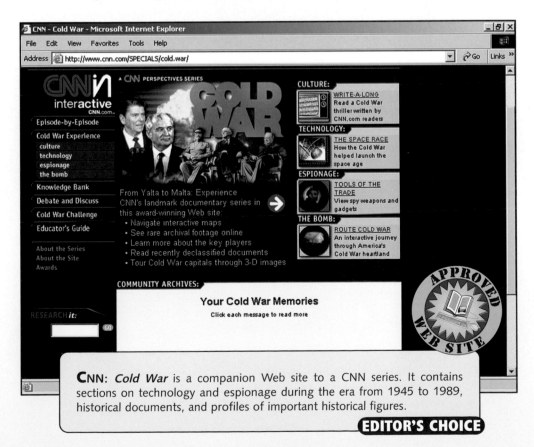

CNN: *Cold War* is a companion Web site to a CNN series. It contains sections on technology and espionage during the era from 1945 to 1989, historical documents, and profiles of important historical figures.

EDITOR'S CHOICE

Agency (NSA) had all spied on Americans. Much of the spying was done without any evidence of wrongdoing or permission from a court.

One program involved opening the mail of people or groups certain officials did not like. Two of these were author John Steinbeck and Senator Edward Kennedy.[6] Other targets were people in groups that were working for peace during the Vietnam War (1957–75). According to the Church Committee, "Opposition to government policy or the

◀ *J. Edgar Hoover was the director of the FBI from 1924 to 1972. It is believed that his dislike for Dr. King led the FBI to investigate the minister.*

expression of controversial views was frequently considered sufficient for collecting data on Americans."[7] This, too, was in direct violation of the U.S. Constitution.

➡ THE PUBLIC REACTION

The report's findings appalled many Americans. They felt that government actions had violated their right to privacy and free speech. Most felt that these rights were vital in a free country. The government is not allowed to spy on people just because they have ideas the government does not like. These are the actions of a dictatorship.

Americans had a long tradition of being fiercely protective of their freedoms. They had defended their liberties many times in the past. Sometimes this meant going to war against other countries.

The Church Committee Report reminded Americans that they had to be just as vigilant about guarding their right to privacy from another kind of attack. This kind came from their own government. Americans believed the United States government must respect their privacy.

The nation's founders had created the Fourth Amendment to the Constitution for just this purpose. They knew from experience that abuses from within one's government could be as menacing as those from the outside.

2 THE HISTORY OF THE FOURTH AMENDMENT

The roots of the Fourth Amendment extend back to the 1700s when America was still under the control of Great Britain. Until that time, Britain's rulers had given the colonists a lot of freedom in governing themselves. They had formed their own governments and developed their own laws. By the 1700s, the Americans had grown accustomed to living by self-rule.

In the mid-1700s, though, King George III began limiting the colonists' freedoms. Several of his new policies restricted rights the colonists had grown used to enjoying. One was the use of writs of assistance.

→WRITS OF ASSISTANCE

A writ of assistance was a permanent search warrant. They were most often granted to customs officials. Customs officials collected taxes on merchandise coming into or going out of the colonies. A writ of assistance gave an official the right to search anyone

BICKERSTAFF's
BOSTON ALMANACK.

For the Year of our LORD 1770; Being the second Year after Leap Year,

The honorable James Otis was a colonial lawyer who fought for the privacy rights of individuals.

The   HON. JAMES OTIS, jun. Esq:

anywhere at anytime. This way the government could be sure that all of America's goods were properly taxed.

Many Americans believed that writs of assistances were abuses of power. Among them was colonial lawyer James Otis. He felt that writs intruded on a person's right to privacy. Otis went to the Massachusetts Superior Court in 1761 to ask that it deny a writ of assistance to a customs official. In a speech before the court, Otis called writs "the worst instrument of arbitrary power." In Otis's view, "a man's house is his castle; and whilst he is quiet, he is well guarded as a prince in his castle."[1] The court issued the writ anyway. Yet Otis's words were not forgotten.

→TAXES AND SMUGGLING

In addition to issuing writs, Great Britain passed new tax laws on the colonists. In 1764 it imposed the Sugar Act. The Sugar Act taxed molasses coming into the colonies from other countries. The colonists used the molasses to make rum.

Rum makers felt the new tax would ruin their business. Some got out of paying taxes by bribing customs officials. Others hid goods from them. Avoiding taxes by hiding goods is called smuggling.

When customs officials found smuggled goods, they took them. This is called seizure. Goods that

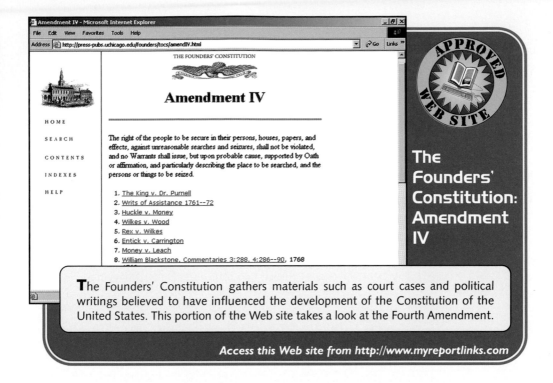

Amendment IV - Microsoft Internet Explorer

File   Edit   View   Favorites   Tools   Help

Address http://press-pubs.uchicago.edu/founders/tocs/amendIV.html   Go   Links »

THE FOUNDERS' CONSTITUTION

Amendment IV

HOME

SEARCH

CONTENTS

INDEXES

HELP

The right of the people to be secure in their persons, houses, papers, and effects, against unreasonable searches and seizures, shall not be violated, and no Warrants shall issue, but upon probable cause, supported by Oath or affirmation, and particularly describing the place to be searched, and the persons or things to be seized.

1. The King v. Dr. Purnell
2. Writs of Assistance 1761--72
3. Huckle v. Money
4. Wilkes v. Wood
5. Rex v. Wilkes
6. Entick v. Carrington
7. Money v. Leach
8. William Blackstone, Commentaries 3:288, 4:286--90, 1768

**The Founders'
Constitution:
Amendment
IV**

The Founders' Constitution gathers materials such as court cases and political writings believed to have influenced the development of the Constitution of the United States. This portion of the Web site takes a look at the Fourth Amendment.

Access this Web site from http://www.myreportlinks.com

were seized were turned over to the British government.

Customs officials were not the only ones who seized goods. The British Royal Navy regularly stopped American merchant ships to search them. When Navy commanders found goods that had not been properly taxed, they, too, seized the merchandise.

As a reward, the British government paid naval commanders and customs officials a bonus for seized goods. This allowed some authorities to make a lot of money through searches and seizures.

Yet the colonists continued to smuggle. The English Parliament reduced the taxes on molasses in

1766. They hoped the lower tax would discourage smuggling. It did not.

In 1767, new taxes were imposed. The Townshend Acts taxed glass, lead, paint, paper, and tea brought into the colonies. To protest these new taxes, Americans stopped buying the British goods.

COLONIAL PROTESTS

British officials were angry that the government was losing money because of the colonists. Some were even more angered by the Americans' defiance of the law. As a result, British authorities encouraged officials to search ships, homes, and businesses as much as possible.

This caused great resentment among the colonists. Some protested against these general searches. A few of the protests led to violence. In one, a New Jersey tax collector was beaten and his son tarred and feathered. During another, an eleven-year-old boy was accidentally shot and killed. Crowds of colonists often gathered at customs offices. Sometimes they destroyed the buildings. Other times they forced officials to stop search operations.

TALK OF REBELLION

The British government responded to the riots by sending more soldiers to America. In October 1774, colonial leaders met in what would become

American patriot Paul Revere created this engraving that depicted his account of the Boston Massacre, in which British soldiers fired into a crowd of unarmed colonists. The Boston Massacre was one incident that led colonists to protest the Quartering Act.

known as the First Continental Congress. At this meeting, the colonial leaders voted to cut off trade with Great Britain until all of the new taxes were abolished. They also created the Continental Army. They wanted to be ready if the colonies needed to defend themselves against the king.

Some colonists talked about revolting against the British government. This gave the British a new reason to search goods and property. Now they looked for plans of rebellion and weapons that could be used in an uprising. By 1775 the British were raiding ships, homes, barns, stores, and warehouses at will.

In May 1775, colonial leaders met for a Second Continental Congress. There had already been fighting between American and British troops, but most colonists still wanted to make peace with England. So leaders listed their complaints in a formal document and sent it to the king. One complaint was the government's use of unlimited search power.

➡ THE REVOLUTIONARY WAR

Great Britain's response did not satisfy the colonists. By 1776 the Americans had decided they could no longer live under British rule. They planned to break with Great Britain and become an independent nation. Leaders agreed that each colony would become a state. These states would join together into one country called the United States of America.

Colonial leaders announced their intentions on July 4 in the Declaration of Independence. The Declaration listed several reasons why the colonists were breaking away from England. One referred to the general searches. It said that King George had "sent hither swarms of officers to harass our people. . . ."[2]

But Great Britain was not going to let go of its colonies without a fight. For the next seven years, colonists battled the British in the Revolutionary War. The war officially ended in 1783, and the United States of America became an independent nation.

➡A New Nation

The new country's government operated under the rules set forth in the Articles of Confederation. But the Articles did not effectively work. So, leaders gathered to create new rules for the nation. They wrote these in a document called the Constitution of the United States.

The Constitution had to be ratified, or approved of, by the states before it could be implemented. Yet many states did not like it. They did not think it was clear enough in defining the rights of individual citizens.

▲ Artist Frederick Girsch created this image of George Washington (left) standing with other leaders of the Continental Army and its allies.

So states sent the Constitution back to the leaders. Along with it they sent over two hundred suggestions for improvements.

➡ THE FOURTH AMENDMENT

James Madison took on the task of condensing all of the suggestions into a handful of statements. Each statement would be an addition, or amendment, to the Constitution. These amendments would list rights the United States government could not take away from its citizens. The list of amendments would be called the Bill of Rights.

Some ideas came up over and over again. One was the people's desire to be protected from general searches. Americans wanted their government to have limitations on search powers. They did not want it to have the right to search anywhere at anytime in the hopes of finding something illegal.

Madison looked at various state constitutions for ideas. Six of them contained statements about arbitrary searches. Madison liked how the Massachusetts state constitution was worded. It protected its citizens from "unreasonable searches and seizures."

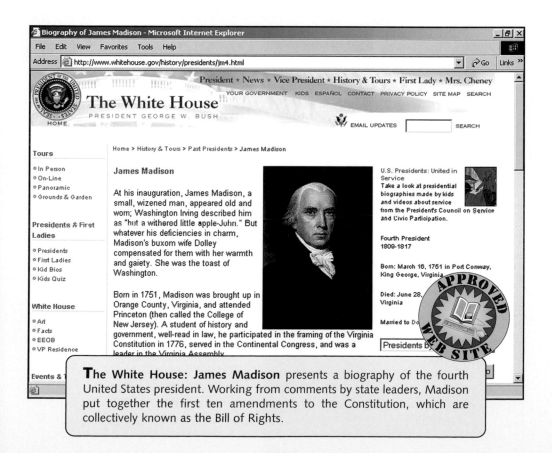

The White House: James Madison presents a biography of the fourth United States president. Working from comments by state leaders, Madison put together the first ten amendments to the Constitution, which are collectively known as the Bill of Rights.

Madison decided to use the phrase, too. His final version read, "The right of the people to be secure in their persons, house, papers, and effects, against unreasonable searches and seizures, shall not be violated and no warrants shall issue, but upon probable cause, supported by oath or affirmation, and particularly describing the place to be searched, and the persons or things to be seized."

When all of the amendments were written, the Bill of Rights was attached to the Constitution and sent back to the states for approval. This time the

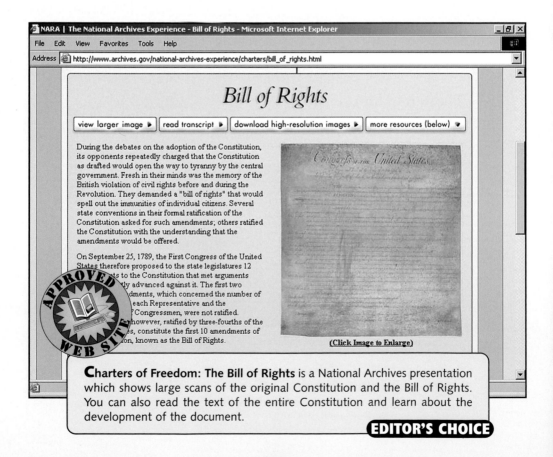

NARA | The National Archives Experience - Bill of Rights - Microsoft Internet Explorer

File   Edit   View   Favorites   Tools   Help

Address http://www.archives.gov/national-archives-experience/charters/bill_of_rights.html

Bill of Rights

view larger image ▶ | read transcript ▶ | download high-resolution images ▶ | more resources (below) ▼

During the debates on the adoption of the Constitution, its opponents repeatedly charged that the Constitution as drafted would open the way to tyranny by the central government. Fresh in their minds was the memory of the British violation of civil rights before and during the Revolution. They demanded a "bill of rights" that would spell out the immunities of individual citizens. Several state conventions in their formal ratification of the Constitution asked for such amendments; others ratified the Constitution with the understanding that the amendments would be offered.

On September 25, 1789, the First Congress of the United States therefore proposed to the state legislatures 12 [amendmen]ts to the Constitution that met arguments [advanced] against it. The first two [amen]dments, which concerned the number of each Representative and the [Congressmen, were not ratified. [however, ratified by three-fourths of the [state]s, constitute the first 10 amendments of [the Constituti]on, known as the Bill of Rights.

(Click Image to Enlarge)

Charters of Freedom: The Bill of Rights is a National Archives presentation which shows large scans of the original Constitution and the Bill of Rights. You can also read the text of the entire Constitution and learn about the development of the document.

EDITOR'S CHOICE

state leaders liked it. The Constitution was ratified by enough states to become the law of the land in 1791.

➔THE LEGISLATIVE BRANCH AND THE EXECUTIVE BRANCH

The United States Constitution outlined a federal government that would share power with the states. To accomplish this, the federal government was divided into three parts called branches.

Each branch had a job. The legislative branch would represent the states. It would be made up of people elected by the citizens of each state. These elected officials would belong to the United States Congress. Congress's job was to make laws for the nation.

The executive branch would enforce these laws. The leader of this part of the government was the president of the United States. The president would also be elected by the people.

➔THE JUDICIAL BRANCH

The third branch the founders created was the judicial branch. The judicial branch would conduct the trials of people accused of breaking federal laws. It would also make sure that federal laws and actions followed the U.S. Constitution. This would be done through a system of federal courts.

At the lowest level would be area, or district courts. People who violated federal laws would be

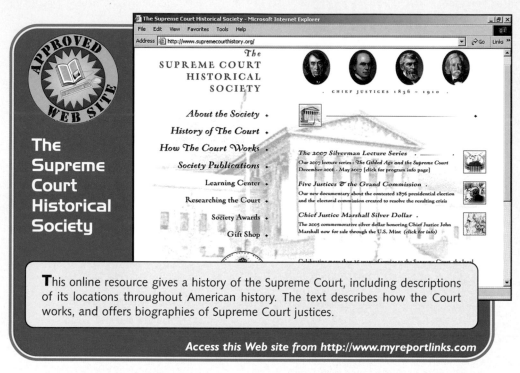

The
Supreme
Court
Historical
Society

This online resource gives a history of the Supreme Court, including descriptions of its locations throughout American history. The text describes how the Court works, and offers biographies of Supreme Court justices.

Access this Web site from http://www.myreportlinks.com

tried in one of these. At the next level were the courts of appeal.

Courts of appeal would judge cases in which people believed that something in their original trial did not follow the Constitution or proper procedure. Once a ruling was made, either side could accept the court's decision or appeal it to a higher court. The highest federal court to hear an appeal was the United States Supreme Court.

➲THE SUPREME COURT

Today the U.S. Supreme Court includes nine judges called justices. These justices listen to cases in which people believe a law or procedure has violated the Constitution. Cases can be brought to the Supreme Court by a person, a group of people, a company, or a governmental body.

Yet the Court does not hear all of the cases it is asked to judge. Each year it chooses only a few to consider from hundreds of requests. Most often these are cases the Court believes will help clarify constitutional questions.

When a case is brought before the Court, the lawyers on each side of the issue go in front of the justices and present their ideas in a speech. These speeches are called arguments. During the arguments, justices ask the lawyers questions.

After a case has been argued, the justices meet and discuss it. They often look back to prior cases with similar issues.

▲ An image of the nine Supreme Court justices taken in 2006. Seated left to right are Anthony M. Kennedy, John Paul Stevens, Chief Justice John G. Roberts, Jr., Antonin Scalia, and David H. Souter. Standing left to right are Stephen G. Breyer, Clarence Thomas, Ruth Bader Ginsburg, and Samuel Alito, Jr.

→SUPREME COURT DECISIONS

Then the justices vote. Justices have two possible ways to vote. They can agree with, or uphold, the original verdict. Or, if they believe the Constitution has been violated, they can reverse the original ruling. Cases that are reversed are sometimes remanded. This means they are sent back to a lower court for review using the boundaries set in the Supreme Court ruling.

The justices' votes are counted, and the majority vote wins. One of the justices who has voted with the majority writes a report about the decision. This report is called an opinion. Sometimes other justices in the majority write an opinion, too. This most often happens when a justice agrees with a ruling, but for different reasons than the ones stated in the majority opinion. This kind of report is called a concurring opinion.

In some cases, the vote is unanimous. Many cases, though, end up in a split vote. Often, one or more justices holds a minority view. This is called dissenting. Any justice with a dissenting view may write a dissenting opinion.

Once the U.S. Supreme Court has ruled on a case, its decision is final. There is no higher court at which to lodge an appeal.

THE MEANING OF THE FOURTH AMENDMENT 3

"The right of the people to be secure in their persons, house, papers, and effects, against unreasonable searches and seizures, shall not be violated and no warrants shall issue, but upon probable cause, supported by oath or affirmation, and particularly describing the place to be searched, and the persons or things to be seized."

➔PROTECTION FROM SEARCHES AND SEIZURES

The Fourth Amendment prevents the government from searching a person's home or belongings simply because it wants to. The amendment says that the government must have a good reason to search through things that are thought of as private.

In addition to searches, the Fourth Amendment addresses seizures. A seizure refers to people as well as to material things. An arrest is the seizure of a person. Arresting a person does not always mean taking someone to a police station. An arrest happens when a legal authority stops an individual for a period of time. The

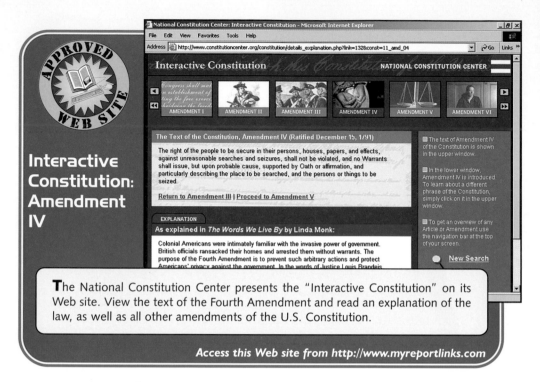

The National Constitution Center presents the "Interactive Constitution" on its Web site. View the text of the Fourth Amendment and read an explanation of the law, as well as all other amendments of the U.S. Constitution.

Access this Web site from http://www.myreportlinks.com

Fourth Amendment says that like searches, seizures can only be done with a good reason.

The Fourth Amendment says it is up to a judge to decide what makes a good reason. A judge must think that a search or seizure has a good chance of finding evidence of a crime. This limits the government's ability to search people or places at will, hoping to find something illegal.

→ THE FIRST PART OF THE AMENDMENT

A close look at the Fourth Amendment shows how it does this. The amendment's first words say that it is protecting "The right of the people to be secure . . ." This means the amendment protects a citizen's right to keep some things private.

The amendment then goes on to list what things citizens have a right to keep private. The first thing listed is person. Person means an individual's physical body and clothing. It includes medical information about a person. Furthermore, it applies to conversations a person believes is private.

The amendment then lists house. This includes a parked recreational vehicle. It has also been extended to include a person's place of work.

Next the amendment lists papers and effects. Papers are personal documents like bank records and letters. Effects are possessions like televisions, furniture, or video games.

According to the Fourth Amendment, all of these places and things are areas where people can expect privacy. In these places, there are limits to the government's search and seizure powers. This does not mean the government cannot search them. It only means that they are protected from "unreasonable" searches and seizures.

Unreasonable is an important word in the amendment. It is what gives the government the right to conduct searches and seizures. It means that the government can search a private area if the search and seizure is conducted in a reasonable manner.

➲THE SECOND PART OF THE AMENDMENT

The second part of the amendment defines what is considered a reasonable manner. It says,

This man was searched and arrested for carrying illegal drugs at his place of business. The Fourth Amendment protects a person from being searched at his or her place of work, but not if the police reasonably suspect that he or she is involved in illegal activity.

". . . no warrants shall issue, but upon probable cause, supported by oath or affirmation, and particularly describing the place to be searched, and the persons or things to be seized."

This part of the amendment sets forth the procedures the government must follow when it wants to search and seize a person or property. First, any of these actions requires a warrant. A warrant is a legal order issued by a court.

⊖ Not Without "Probable Cause"

To obtain a warrant for a search, a law enforcement official must go before a judge. The officer must swear under oath why he or she believes that a specific person has committed a crime. The officer must then tell the judge what evidence of the crime is believed to be located where. This sworn statement is called an affidavit.

The Fourth Amendment says that an affidavit must be specific about the area to be searched. For example, it might say an officer believes stolen televisions "are being kept in the garage of the house at 1226 Oak Street."

Once a judge has heard all of an officer's testimony, the judge must make a decision. If he or she is convinced that evidence of a crime might be found, the judge can issue a warrant. This warrant must describe the place or person to be searched as well as what is to be seized.

Police are then permitted to search in that place and take what is specified. They cannot go beyond the boundaries of the warrant. For

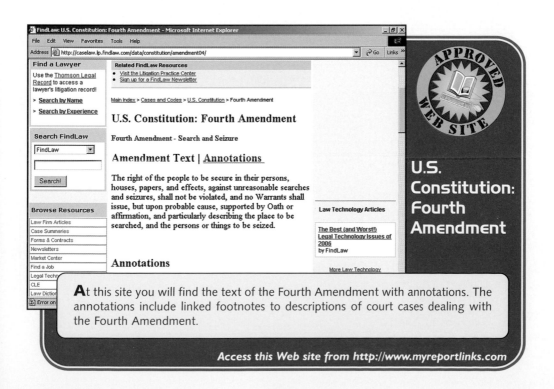

At this site you will find the text of the Fourth Amendment with annotations. The annotations include linked footnotes to descriptions of court cases dealing with the Fourth Amendment.

Access this Web site from http://www.myreportlinks.com

instance, the officers looking for stolen televisions could not look in drawers or toolboxes. Televisions could not be in these places. Specific words protect citizens from general searches such as the ones conducted in the colonies using writs of assistance.

The Fourth Amendment also gives judges guidance in issuing warrants. It says that no warrants should be issued unless there is "probable cause." This means that an affidavit must cause a judge to think there is a good probability that a search or seizure will turn up evidence of a crime. Probable cause was the level of certainty the nation's founders wanted the government to have before conducting a search.

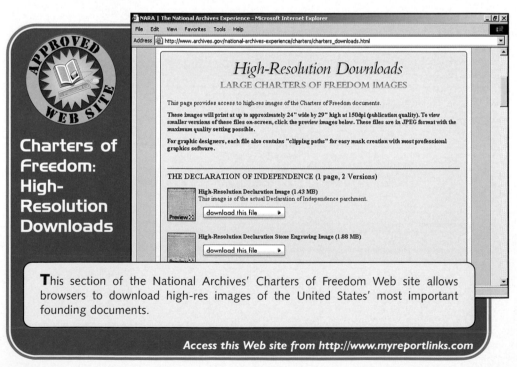

Charters of Freedom: High-Resolution Downloads

This section of the National Archives' Charters of Freedom Web site allows browsers to download high-res images of the United States' most important founding documents.

Access this Web site from http://www.myreportlinks.com

⇒INTERPRETING THE AMENDMENT

Even after analyzing the amendment, though, experts find its wording a little vague. It does not list specific situations in which a warrant should be granted to conduct a search. It does not define the words "reasonable" or "probable cause." Yet the general wording has been beneficial to society.

Listing every situation in which to issue a warrant would be impossible. Each situation is different. Furthermore, the nation's founders could not have anticipated the developments and inventions that would one day impact the search and seizure amendment. For example, they had no idea how future doctors would be able to check the blood for illegal drug use. The general wording of the amendment has allowed society to make needed adjustments.

The founders crafted a court system for making these adjustments. Federal courts would judge varying opinions about the Constitution. They would settle questions in a peaceful manner while protecting society and a person's Constitutional rights.

Since 1791, the Supreme Court has heard many cases involving the Fourth Amendment. As a result, it has issued several general principles about what the amendment allows and requires. These principles are called precedents.

Precedents create guidelines for judges of lower courts to follow when deciding the Fourth

Amendment cases that come before them. The Supreme Court often uses its own precedents when deciding cases. This is known as *stare decisis*. There are times, however, when the Supreme Court rejects, or overrules, a precedent.

→EXCEPTIONS TO THE AMENDMENT

Some of the most important Fourth Amendment precedents have been about exceptions to it. The Court has ruled that in some situations it is not necessary for a law enforcement official to obtain a warrant before making a search.

The reason is usually because seeking a warrant takes time. Police must find a judge and explain evidence. In some situations, there is no time to do this and still protect the public. For example, if a man claims to have set a bomb in his office to

◄ This person is being frisked by police. Law enforcement officers are always allowed to search a suspect to ensure that the person is not carrying a weapon.

explode in ten minutes, it would not be practical for the police to go to a judge, swear out an affidavit, and get a warrant before searching the office and seizing the bomb.

The Supreme Court has ruled that warrants are not needed in situations like these. They require immediate action. These situations are called crisis situations.

➔ CRISIS SITUATIONS

One kind of crisis situation involves safety issues. All arrests have the possibility of becoming dangerous.

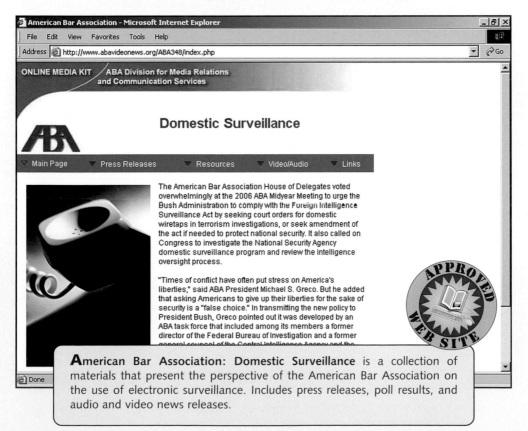

American Bar Association – Microsoft Internet Explorer

File   Edit   View   Favorites   Tools   Help

Address http://www.abavideonews.org/ABA348/index.php

ONLINE MEDIA KIT   ABA Division for Media Relations and Communication Services

Domestic Surveillance

ABA

▽ Main Page   ▼ Press Releases   ▼ Resources   ▼ Video/Audio   ▼ Links

The American Bar Association House of Delegates voted overwhelmingly at the 2006 ABA Midyear Meeting to urge the Bush Administration to comply with the Foreign Intelligence Surveillance Act by seeking court orders for domestic wiretaps in terrorism investigations, or seek amendment of the act if needed to protect national security. It also called on Congress to investigate the National Security Agency domestic surveillance program and review the intelligence oversight process.

"Times of conflict have often put stress on America's liberties," said ABA President Michael S. Greco. But he added that asking Americans to give up their liberties for the sake of security is a "false choice." In transmitting the new policy to President Bush, Greco pointed out it was developed by an ABA task force that included among its members a former director of the Federal Bureau of Investigation and a former general counsel of the Central Intelligence Agency and the

Done

American **Bar** **Association:** **Domestic** **Surveillance** is a collection of materials that present the perspective of the American Bar Association on the use of electronic surveillance. Includes press releases, poll results, and audio and video news releases.

Suspects being arrested may have weapons and be desperate to escape. Therefore, officers are always allowed to search a suspect who is put under arrest to make sure the suspect does not have a weapon. These searches are called searches incident to arrest. Searches incident to arrest can be made without warrants.

There are other kinds of searches that can be done without a warrant in the interest of safety. Certain employees can be required to have a drug test without a warrant. These are people who

▲ The Supreme Court has ruled that police can search a person's vehicle if the officers have "reasonable suspicion" that a crime has been committed.

work in jobs that make them responsible for the safety of others. For example, bus drivers and airline pilots can be tested for drug use without a warrant.

Other crisis situations arise from the need to enforce laws effectively. The Court realizes that the delay in obtaining a warrant may make a search useless. While police are seeking a warrant, a suspect can be destroying evidence of a crime. Therefore, police may search without a warrant if there is a chance evidence will be destroyed. This kind of search is often done incident to arrest.

Another exception to the warrant clause arises when police are chasing a suspect. Police are allowed to follow a suspect into a house even though they have no warrant to enter. This is called hot pursuit.

⊜OTHER EXCEPTIONS

A law officer does not need a warrant if a suspect gives his or her consent to a search. Even a house can be searched without a warrant if someone in the house gives police permission to do so. Furthermore, police are allowed to seize illegal objects that are in plain view without a warrant.

Police can stop and question airline passengers without a warrant if the passenger acts like someone who is carrying drugs to sell. In addition, searches by customs officials at the country's borders can be done without a warrant.

The Supreme Court has been careful to note that all of these exceptions are only exceptions to getting a warrant. They are not exceptions to the need for probable cause. This means that in each exception, the police making a search or seizure must have probable cause to think that a crime has been committed.

The Court has made these exceptions clear by saying that the Fourth Amendment was not meant to help criminals get around the law.[1] It was written to protect people from general evidence gathering expeditions.

→ THE EXPECTATION OF PRIVACY

In order to decide Fourth Amendment cases, the Supreme Court has had to create a legal definition of the word "search." Is every hunt through items by the police a Fourth Amendment search?

The Court has decided that a legal search occurs when police look through things that people have a reasonable expectation to keep private. For example, when people put their trash at the street to be collected, they have no expectation that this trash is private. Therefore, police can look through it without a warrant.

Furthermore, the Court has ruled that people have no expectation of privacy when they are engaged in an illegal activity. If drug-sniffing dogs reveal illegal drugs in a person's briefcase, for

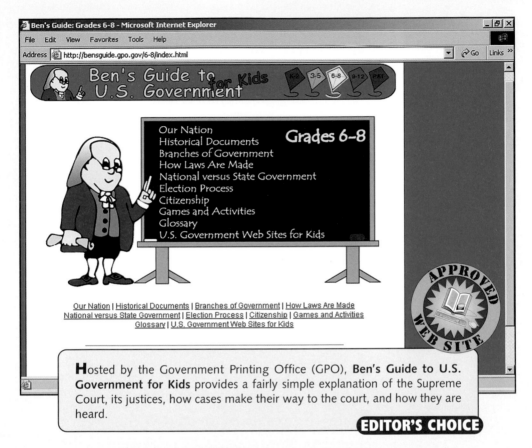

File   Edit   View   Favorites   Tools   Help

Address http://bensguide.gpo.gov/6-8/index.html   Go   Links »

Ben's Guide to U.S. Government for Kids   K-2   3-5   6-8   9-12   Parent

Our Nation
Historical Documents   **Grades 6-8**
Branches of Government
How Laws Are Made
National versus State Government
Election Process
Citizenship
Games and Activities
Glossary
U.S. Government Web Sites for Kids

Our Nation | Historical Documents | Branches of Government | How Laws Are Made
National versus State Government | Election Process | Citizenship | Games and Activities
Glossary | U.S. Government Web Sites for Kids

Hosted by the Government Printing Office (GPO), **Ben's Guide to U.S. Government for Kids** provides a fairly simple explanation of the Supreme Court, its justices, how cases make their way to the court, and how they are heard.

EDITOR'S CHOICE

instance, the police do not need a warrant to search the case.

➔THE SUPREME COURT AS REFEREE

One of the most important protections the Fourth Amendment gives United States citizens is its requirement that a judge decide if there can be a search or seizure. A judge serves as an independent observer and creates a shield between police and citizens. This keeps police from becoming overly eager in performing their job and violating citizens' privacy rights.

When reviewing Fourth Amendment cases, the Supreme Court is not deciding on the guilt or innocence of the person being tried. The Court is determining whether law enforcement officials and judges have followed correct procedures while investigating a crime, making an arrest, and conducting a trial. The Supreme Court acts as a kind of referee between law enforcement and the Constitution. Its job is to make sure that everyone follows the rules.

While deciding how the Constitution applies to various cases, justices often think about the original intent of the Fourth Amendment. They try to rule cases based on what the nation's founders had in mind when creating the amendment. Today's Fourth Amendment understandings and procedures are the result of over two hundred years of thought by Supreme Court justices.

THE FOURTH AMENDMENT IN COURT: 1800–1968

*T*he first Supreme Court case to impact the Fourth Amendment was actually about the Fifth Amendment. However, the case of *Barron* v. *City of Baltimore* (1833) ended up having an affect on all of the amendments, including the Fourth.

John Barron brought this case before the Court. He believed the city of Baltimore had violated his constitutional rights. A city street construction project had ruined business at Barron's seaside wharf. He charged that the city had not properly compensated him for destroying his livelihood. This, he said, was a violation of the Fifth Amendment. It says that the government cannot take private property without paying for it.

John Marshall was the fourth chief justice ▶
of the Supreme Court. He gave the majority
opinion in the case Barron v. Baltimore.

But the Supreme Court ruled against Barron. It said that the U.S. Constitution and its amendments did not apply to cities or states. It only applied to actions taken by the federal government. The Court said that cities and states had their own laws. Therefore, the Court said, the Constitution did not protect Barron from the actions of the city of Baltimore. Complaints about it had to be made in a city or state court.

THE FOURTEENTH AMENDMENT

This idea applied to all of the rights listed in the Constitution. The Court ruled that these rights were written to safeguard citizens from the actions of the federal government. Each state could make its own laws. This meant that the Fourth Amendment only applied to searches and seizures carried out by the federal government.

This precedent was used until after the Civil War. When the war ended in 1865, some states did not treat newly freed slaves as equal citizens. They created laws called Black Codes that limited their rights. In order to stop this practice, Congress wrote a new amendment.

The Fourteenth Amendment was added to the Constitution in 1868. It said that all former slaves were now United States citizens. All states had to honor their new status and give African Americans the same fundamental rights as everyone else.

UNIVERSITY of LOUISVILLE
dare to be great

Louis D. Brandeis
SCHOOL OF LAW LIBRARY

Library Home
General Information
Circulation
Student Services
Faculty & Staff
Library Maps
Special Collections
Research
How Do I Find?

Copyright © 2004
Law Library
Brandeis School of Law,
University of Louisville.
PH: (502) 852-6392
FAX:(502)
All rights re

THE RIGHT TO PRIVACY by
Samuel Warren and Louis D.
Brandeis

Originally published in *4 Harvard
Law Review 193 (1890)*

"It could be done only on principles of private justice, moral fitness, and public
convenience, which, when applied to a new subject, make common law without a
precedent; much more when received and approved by usage."

Willes, J., in *Millar v. Taylor*, 4 Burr, 2303, 2312.

That the individual shall have full protection in person and in property is a principle
as old as the common law; but it has been found necessary from time to time to
define anew the exact nature and extent of such protection. Political, social, and
economic changes entail the recognition of new rights, and the common law, in its

"The Right
to Privacy"
by Samuel
Warren and
Louis D.
Brandeis

Originally published in 1890 by the *Harvard Law Review*, this article was very important in the development of privacy rights. Brandeis later served on the Supreme Court.

Access this Web site from http://www.myreportlinks.com

This was the first time the federal government said that states had to guarantee its citizens certain rights. This is called incorporating rights against the states. Yet the Fourteenth Amendment did not specify which rights were fundamental and had to be incorporated. Future court cases would have to define these.

→THE EXCLUSIONARY RULE

In 1914, a case came before the Court that created a precedent called the Exclusionary Rule. The Exclusionary Rule would become one of the most debated Fourth Amendment precedents. It arose out of a case called *Weeks* v. *U.S.* (1914).

In the case of Weeks v. The United States, Freemont Weeks was arrested after the police used a hidden key to get into his house. The Supreme Court ruled that this was a violation of Weeks's Fourth Amendment rights.

The case began when Kansas City police officers arrested Freemont Weeks while he was at work. They charged him with using the United States mail to transport lottery tickets. This was a violation of federal law.

As Weeks was being arrested, other police officers went to his house. They located a hidden key and entered. Although they did not have a warrant, they searched Weeks's home for evidence of his crimes. Federal officials arrived later and searched further. They found letters, papers, and other items. Many were used at Weeks's trial to help convict him.

Weeks appealed his conviction. He believed that law enforcement agents should have had a warrant before entering his home and seizing his property. His case ended up in the Supreme Court.

The Court agreed with Weeks. It went on to say that because the police did not have a warrant, any evidence seized in their search could not be used in his trial.

⇒ DEBATING THIS NEW RULE

This ruling set a new precedent. It said that evidence seized in violation of Fourth Amendment procedures could not be used as evidence in a federal court. This precedent became known as the Exclusionary Rule. The Exclusionary Rule did not mean that illegal searches would automatically set a suspect free. It only meant that any evidence obtained illegally could not be used in the suspect's trial.

The Court believed the Exclusionary Rule would keep police from violating the Fourth Amendment. Police would have no reason to search without a warrant if the evidence they found could not be used in a trial. Therefore, police would want to seek out a warrant before making a search. The Court felt the Exclusionary Rule would protect an individual's privacy the way the nation's founders had intended.

Yet not everyone liked the Exclusionary Rule. Some people argued that it was irrational. They said that the damage to a person's rights had already been done by improper procedure. Excluding evidence from a trial would not change that. They believed that all evidence should be allowed. Many future court cases would test the limits of the Exclusionary Rule. None, though, would eliminate it.

⊘CAR SEARCHES

Carroll v. *U.S.* (1925) was one early test of the Exclusionary Rule. It was also the

Prohibition agents nab a bootlegger on the streets of ▶ *Washington, D.C. The Supreme Court allowed these types of searches as the outcome of a case called* Carroll *v. U.S.*

first Supreme Court case involving a car search. This case arose from a violation of Prohibition laws. The Eighteenth Amendment made the sale of alcoholic beverages in the United States illegal. People who sold liquor illegally were known as bootleggers.

Carroll v. *U.S.* began when law officials were patrolling a highway that ran from Canada to Grand Rapids, Michigan. This highway was commonly used by bootleggers to pick up liquor in Canada for sale in the United States.

While on patrol, the officers saw two men they had previously suspected of selling alcohol. They believed there was a good chance the men were transporting liquor. The officers stopped the driver and searched the car. Inside they found several bottles of whiskey and seized it to use as evidence.

⇒MOBILITY MEANS LESS PROTECTION

George Carroll and John Kiro were convicted of violating Prohibition laws. They appealed, saying that the officers had no probable cause to stop them. Furthermore, they said, the officers had no warrant to search the car, and no authority to seize the liquor. Under the Exclusionary Rule, then, this evidence should have been excluded from trial.

The Supreme Court decided differently. It said that because the law officials had prior suspicions about the men, they had probable cause to stop them. The Court said this gave them the right to search the car. The Court ruled that automobiles could be searched without a warrant when law authorities had probable cause.

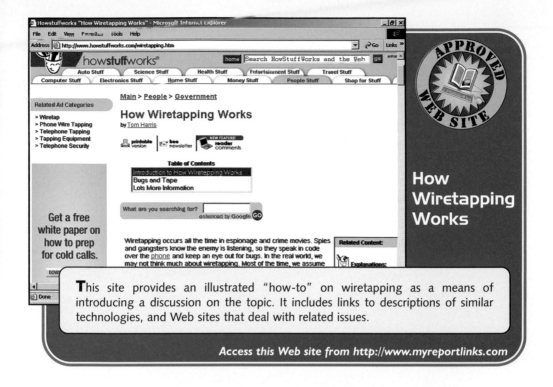

This site provides an illustrated "how-to" on wiretapping as a means of introducing a discussion on the topic. It includes links to descriptions of similar technologies, and Web sites that deal with related issues.

Access this Web site from http://www.myreportlinks.com

The Court gave several reasons for allowing such searches. First, cars are mobile. While officers are seeking a warrant, cars can be driving off and disposing of illegal substances. Furthermore, automobile windows allow outsiders to easily look inside. People inside a car, therefore, should expect less privacy than people inside a home. Finally, the Court believed that the government had an interest in regulating cars. The safety of the public partly depended on the safe use of automobiles.

All of these reasons led the Court to conclude that automobiles deserved a low degree of protection from the Fourth Amendment. This meant that police had fewer restrictions when searching them

than they had when searching people or homes.
This concept would affect rulings for years to come.

⊖WIRETAPPING AND THE FOURTH AMENDMENT

At about the same time, the telephone was making
its way into everyday life in America. It would
create new questions about privacy and the Fourth
Amendment.

Shortly after the telephone was invented,
scientists began devising ways to eavesdrop elec-
tronically on telephone conversations. This was
called wiretapping, or tapping, a telephone line.

▲ Law enforcement officers conducting wiretaps or other forms of electronic
eavesdropping would record conversations on a reel-to-reel tape recorder.

Other types of electronic eavesdropping devices were also being invented. These could be hidden from view and wired to listening devices in other locations. They gave police the ability to secretly listen from a distance to conversations held in another place.

At times police used one of these electronic devices to find evidence of a crime. But some people questioned whether or not this was legal. Should people expect telephone conversations to be private? What about a conversation with a friend? Was electronic eavesdropping a search? If so, should the Fourth Amendment be applied to these kinds of searches?

➡EAVESDROPPING AND THE FOURTH AMENDMENT

The case of *Olmstead* v. *U.S.* (1928) addressed this issue. It involved Roy Olmstead who was also suspected of violating prohibition laws. Federal agents hoped to gain evidence against him by tapping the telephone in his home, office, and the homes of his business partners. The wiretapping work did not require going into any of the suspects' personal spaces. None of it was done with a warrant.

Evidence was gathered and Olmstead was convicted. But he appealed his conviction. Olmstead believed that the Fourth Amendment protected him from electronic eavesdropping without a warrant. Therefore, he said, this evidence should have been excluded at his trial.

The Supreme Court, however, upheld Olmstead's conviction in a 5–4 decision. The majority of justices believed that electronic eavesdropping was not restricted by the Fourth Amendment. They felt that as long as there was no invasion into a dwelling, the surveillance was neither a search nor a seizure. Chief Justice William Howard Taft wrote in the majority opinion that the Fourth Amendment only applied to material things.

Yet several justices disagreed. Among them was Justice Louis Brandeis. He wrote a dissenting opinion. In it he said that the nation's founders meant to protect ". . . the right to be let alone . . . To protect, that right, every

William Howard Taft was the ▶
twenty-seventh president of the
United States, and later served as
Chief Justice of the Supreme Court.

unjustifiable intrusion by the government upon the privacy of the individual, whatever the means employed, must be deemed a violation of the Fourth Amendment."[1]

Brandeis, however, held a minority opinion, and the precedent was set. For many years, law authorities were allowed to eavesdrop with electronic devices as long as they did not go into, or penetrate, a person's physical space.

PROBABLE CAUSE

The next important Fourth Amendment case to come before the Supreme Court was *Brinegar* v. *U.S.* (1949). In this case the Court tried to set some guidelines for determining probable cause. It said that the purpose of probable cause was to safeguard citizens from unreasonable violations of privacy. But probable cause could not be so difficult to meet that law enforcement agents could not protect people.

The Court said that when police or judges have to decide whether evidence rises to the level of probable cause, they must ". . . deal with probabilities. These are not technical; they are the factual and practical considerations of everyday life on which reasonable and prudent men, not legal technicians, act."[2] In other words, probable cause could not be neatly defined with any kind of a formula. It could only be determined by applying common sense and logic to a variety of situations.

→ INCORPORATION OF THE EXCLUSIONARY RULE

Another ruling that year would test whether or not the Fourth Amendment should be incorporated against the states. In *Wolf* v. *Colorado* (1949), Julius A. Wolf was charged with illegally performing abortions. He was convicted in a Colorado court with evidence that had been gathered without obtaining a warrant. Wolf believed this violated his Fourth Amendment rights. He appealed his case to the Colorado Supreme Court. It upheld his conviction.

Wolf then took his case to the U.S. Supreme Court. He wanted it to rule on whether or not evidence obtained illegally could be admitted in a state court. In other words, should the Exclusionary Rule be incorporated against the states?

In its ruling, the Supreme Court said that all states had to abide by the Fourth Amendment. But, the Court said, they did not have to follow the Exclusionary Rule.

The Court reasoned that the Exclusionary Rule was a remedy it created to encourage federal officials to follow the Fourth Amendment. The Court said that while all law officers were required to follow Fourth Amendment procedures, each state could devise its own remedy for those who did not.

Some states might want to use the Exclusionary Rule. Others might choose another remedy such as disciplining officers who did not follow proper procedure. As for the federal government, it chose exclusion. Justice Frankfurter delivered the opinion of the Court which ruled that the Exclusionary Rule was not incorporated against the states, and it upheld Wolf's conviction.

➡ OVERTURNING A PRECEDENT

Twelve years later, the Supreme Court overruled this precedent in *Mapp* v. *Ohio* (1961). Dollree

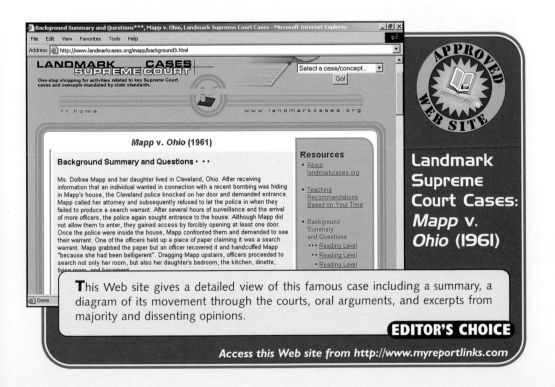

Landmark Supreme Court Cases: Mapp v. Ohio (1961)

This Web site gives a detailed view of this famous case including a summary, a diagram of its movement through the courts, oral arguments, and excerpts from majority and dissenting opinions.

EDITOR'S CHOICE

Access this Web site from http://www.myreportlinks.com

Mapp was suspected of several illegal activities, including harboring a fugitive. This means helping someone hide who has been accused of a crime. Police entered her house without a valid search warrant and found obscene pictures there.

Mapp was found guilty in an Ohio court of possession of obscene materials. She appealed her case to the Supreme Court. Mapp believed that the Ohio law violated her First Amendment right to the freedom of expression.

The Court, however, was not interested in evaluating this idea. Instead, it wanted to revisit its earlier precedent about the Exclusionary Rule. The Court believed that the police did not have a proper warrant to search Mapp's home. Consequently, the evidence that helped convict her was gathered against Fourth Amendment procedures.

To Whom Does the Exclusionary Rule Apply?

In a 6–3 vote, the Court ruled that because of this, the evidence should have been excluded from Mapp's trial. In other words, the Court was saying that the state should have applied the Exclusionary Rule. Mapp's conviction was reversed, and the case remanded.

This ruling directly contradicted the earlier precedent set in *Wolf* v. *Colorado*. In it, the Court had said that the Exclusionary Rule did not apply

When law enforcement officials are working on a case, they need to follow certain standards while gathering evidence. Otherwise, the evidence may not be able to be used at trial and a guilty person could go free.

to the states. But now the Supreme Court believed it should.

In a concurring opinion, Justice Douglas noted that the prior ruling in *Wolf* v. *Colorado* was "not the voice of reason or principle . . ."[3] He went on to say that when the Supreme Court said that the Exclusionary Rule did not apply to the states, it robbed "the Fourth Amendment of much meaningful force."[4]

By incorporating the Exclusionary Rule against the states, the Court was saying that all law enforcement officials had to follow certain standards when gathering evidence. This ruling gave the federal government more power than ever before in deciding how state and local police did their work.

→THE AGUILAR TEST

In *Aguilar* v. *Texas* (1964), the Supreme Court set some boundaries on probable cause. Aguilar had been convicted in a Texas court on drug charges. The warrant used to search his home was obtained based on information from a citizen. A citizen who gives police information about a crime is known as an informant.

This particular informant told police that Aguilar had drugs. But the police affidavit gave no specific information about the informant. It only said that an officer had "received reliable information from a credible person . . ."[5]

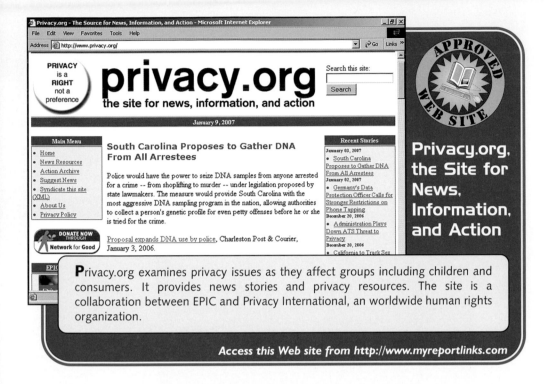

Access this Web site from http://www.myreportlinks.com

Aguilar's lawyers argued that the officer had not given the judge enough information to create probable cause. The affidavit should have had some kind of information about the informant. For example, it should have explained how he or she came upon the tip given to the police.

In this case, the question before the Court was whether the judge should have issued a warrant with no information about the informant. Should police have to supply facts that show an informant is reliable or credible? Or is an officer's belief in the informant enough to rise to the level of probable cause? The Court decided it was not. It reversed and remanded Aguilar's conviction.

Electronic eavesdropping and surveillance require a warrant, but only in places where a person expects privacy. That does not include the monitoring of open rooms or spaces.

This ruling set forth a standard for judges to use when dealing with tips coming from informants. It said that to meet probable cause, an affidavit must contain some information about why an informant should be believed. This new standard became known as the Aguilar test.

➔ ANOTHER OVERTURNED PRECEDENT

In 1967, the Court overturned another one of its prior decisions. In the case of *Katz* v. *U.S.* (1967), FBI agents suspected Charles Katz of placing bets for people and then paying them off. This is called bookmaking. Bookmaking from one state to another is illegal under federal law. Officials suspected that Katz was telephoning bets between Los Angeles, Miami, and Boston.

Federal agents had observed Katz making telephone calls from a booth on the street. So the agents placed listening and recording devices on the outside of the booth in an attempt to gather evidence. They did not have a warrant. Transcripts from the telephone conversations helped convict Katz of illegal activities.

Katz appealed his conviction, saying that a telephone booth was a "constitutionally protected area." He believed police could not invade his privacy there without a warrant.

The lawyers for the government argued that law enforcement officials had followed the principles

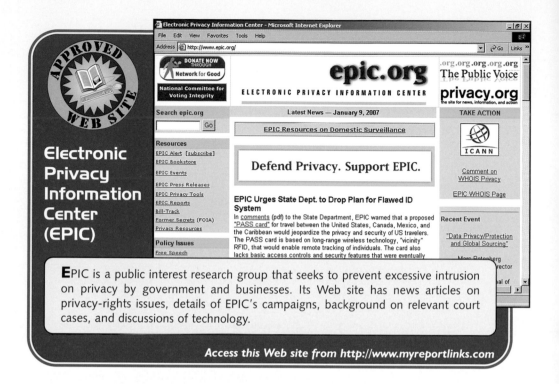

Electronic Privacy Information Center (EPIC)

EPIC is a public interest research group that seeks to prevent excessive intrusion on privacy by government and businesses. Its Web site has news articles on privacy-rights issues, details of EPIC's campaigns, background on relevant court cases, and discussions of technology.

Access this Web site from http://www.myreportlinks.com

set forth in *Olmstead* v. *U.S.* (1928). This case had allowed electronic eavesdropping without a warrant if it did not physically penetrate an individual's space. In Katz's case, the listening device was attached to the outside of a telephone booth. Therefore, it did not invade any personal areas.

The Court, however, decided that the ruling in the Olmstead case had been too narrow when it said that a search only involved tangible material. The Court now believed that the Fourth Amendment should restrict electronic eavesdropping, no matter how it was done.

In the opinion, Justice Potter Stewart noted that a "person inside a telephone booth may rely upon the protection of the Fourth Amendment." Someone who has a conversation there is entitled "to assume that the words he utters into the mouthpiece will not be broadcast to the world."[6]

The Court ruled that wiretapping and electronic eavesdropping were searches and seizures. Therefore, they required warrants. The Court rejected the notion of a "constitutionally protected area." Instead, it ruled that the Fourth Amendment protected people, not areas. It said, "Wherever a man may be, he is entitled to know that he will remain free from unreasonable searches and seizures."[7]

TITLE III

The Court went on to say that if citizens have an expectation of privacy, they are entitled to it. This created guidelines for a legal search. The Court believed that a legal search took place when law enforcement authorities intruded into areas where people had a reasonable "expectation of privacy."

Some people believed the ruling in this case would hinder law enforcement efforts. So Congress passed a law in 1968 called Title III. It was one of many laws in the Federal Omnibus Crime Control Act. Title III gave police the authority to use electronic wiretaps without a warrant if one of the people involved in the conversation gave permission to be listened to and recorded.

Police have the right to frisk citizens when they have good reason to believe that the public is in danger. A good example of this is during a riot.

➔REASONABLE SUSPICION

That same year the Court ruled on the case of *Terry* v. *Ohio* (1968). This case began when police officer Martin McFadden was patrolling an area of Cleveland. He noticed two men walking up and down the street, staring into the same store window time after time. After awhile, a third man joined them. McFadden suspected the men were getting ready to rob the store.

He approached the men, identified himself, and asked them who they were. They whispered to each other, and one man said something to McFadden. McFadden then grabbed the man and patted him down. He found a pistol in his overcoat pocket. McFadden searched the other men and found another gun. He arrested the two men for carrying concealed weapons.

John Terry and Richard Chilton were both convicted. However, they believed that there had been no probable cause to arrest them. This gave McFadden no reason to search them. Their guns, they reasoned, should fall under the Exclusionary Rule.

Government lawyers argued that McFadden's search of the men was incident to arrest. This, they believed, made the search legal.

The Court did not agree. It said there was not enough probable cause for McFadden to arrest the men. Therefore, the argument that the search was incident to arrest was not a good one.

However, the Court went on, there was enough evidence to lead an "experienced, prudent police-man to suspect that Terry was about to engage in burglary or robbery."[8] In this situation, McFadden was protecting himself and others from possible violence. So even though he lacked probable cause to make an arrest, he had a good reason to stop and search the men without a warrant.

The Court ruled that police could stop and frisk citizens when they had a good reason to suspect that lives might be in danger. A frisk is a quick search of a person's clothing. In this particular case, McFadden had that fear. The Court upheld the men's convictions.

With this ruling, the Court created a new "good reason" for conducting a warrantless search. It was called "reasonable suspicion." This new standard said that police could stop and frisk a person without probable cause when police had a reasonable suspicion of danger to themselves or others.

THE FOURTH AMENDMENT IN COURT: 1969–2000

5

*L*ater Fourth Amendment cases addressed many of the same issues as the early cases. For example, in *Spinelli* v. *U.S.* (1969), the Court looked at informant tips again. Its ruling set a new standard for probable cause for tips. The Court described the new standard as a "two-pronged test."

For the first "tip of the prong," a law enforcement officer had to tell a judge how an informant got the information. For the second "tip of the prong," the officer had to provide facts proving the reliability of the informant's report.

For example, an affidavit might say that an informant told an officer she had heard two women bragging about committing a crime. Furthermore, the woman had given this officer information leading to evidence before. This "two-pronged" standard for meeting probable cause became known as the Aguilar-Spinelli test.

⮕SEARCHES INCIDENT TO ARREST

The Supreme Court ruled on another Fourth Amendment case in 1969. This one would set limits on

A man on trial stands before a judge. The Supreme Court decided that police need to pass a "two-pronged" test before a judge could issue a warrant. Otherwise, the case could get thrown out when it gets to court.

the physical area police could search incident to an arrest.

The case of *Chimel* v. *California* (1969) began with police suspicions that Ted Steven Chimel had robbed a coin shop. He was arrested in his home. Then, without a warrant, the police searched his house, attic, garage, and workshop. They found various pieces of evidence in these places. Some was used to convict him of robbery.

Chimel appealed his conviction to the Supreme Court. He believed the search through his property had been illegal. This meant that any evidence found there should have been excluded from trial. The Supreme Court agreed. It said the scope of the Chimel search was unreasonable. In the opinion, Justice Potter Stewart noted that the search "went beyond petitioner's person and the area from within which he might have obtained a weapon or something that could have been used as evidence against him."[1]

This ruling set a precedent that defined the physical area police could search relating to an arrest. It said that this area extended only to the suspect and the areas within the suspect's control or reach.

This decision emphasized to police the purpose of a search incident to arrest. The Court had long recognized that these searches were necessary for the safety of the suspect, the officer, and the public.

It also knew they were important ways to preserve evidence. Such a search, then, could not be done in an area beyond a suspect's reach. This made the searching of Chimel's house improper. His conviction was reversed.

⊖EAVESDROPPING AND BUGS

Soon the Supreme Court was again dealing with issues resulting from advances in technology. Over the decades, eavesdropping devices had become small and powerful. Some used radio waves, making wires unnecessary. This meant they could easily be hidden under a person's clothing. Many people referred to these small eavesdropping devices as bugs.

In *U.S.* v. *White* (1971), the Court decided that a law enforcement agent could wear a hidden bug and record a suspected criminal without a warrant. The Court ruled that when people talk about their own illegal activities, they have no reasonable expectation of privacy. Furthermore, the Court noted, Title III already allowed authorities to secretly tape conversations when one party gave consent. In these situations, the police officer would be the consenting party.

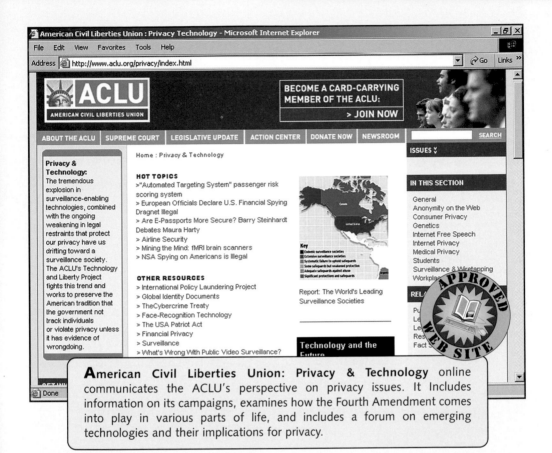

American Civil Liberties Union: Privacy Technology - Microsoft Internet Explorer

File   Edit   View   Favorites   Tools   Help

Address http://www.aclu.org/privacy/index.html

ACLU
AMERICAN CIVIL LIBERTIES UNION

BECOME A CARD-CARRYING
MEMBER OF THE ACLU:
> JOIN NOW

ABOUT THE ACLU | SUPREME COURT | LEGISLATIVE UPDATE | ACTION CENTER | DONATE NOW | NEWSROOM   SEARCH

ISSUES

Home : Privacy & Technology

**Privacy &
Technology:**
The tremendous
explosion in
surveillance-enabling
technologies, combined
with the ongoing
weakening in legal
restraints that protect
our privacy have us
drifting toward a
surveillance society.
The ACLU's Technology
and Liberty Project
fights this trend and
works to preserve the
American tradition that
the government not
track individuals
or violate privacy unless
it has evidence of
wrongdoing.

HOT TOPICS
>"Automated Targeting System" passenger risk
scoring system
> European Officials Declare U.S. Financial Spying
Dragnet Illegal
> Are E-Passports More Secure? Barry Steinhardt
Debates Maura Harty
> Airline Security
> Mining the Mind: fMRI brain scanners
> NSA Spying on Americans is Illegal

OTHER RESOURCES
> International Policy Laundering Project
> Global Identity Documents
> TheCybercrime Treaty
> Face-Recognition Technology
> The USA Patriot Act
> Financial Privacy
> Surveillance
> What's Wrong With Public Video Surveillance?

Report: The World's Leading
Surveillance Societies

IN THIS SECTION
General
Anonymity on the Web
Consumer Privacy
Genetics
Internet Free Speech
Internet Privacy
Medical Privacy
Students
Surveillance & Wiretapping
Workplace

**Technology and the
Future**

Done

American Civil Liberties Union: Privacy & Technology online
communicates the ACLU's perspective on privacy issues. It Includes
information on its campaigns, examines how the Fourth Amendment comes
into play in various parts of life, and includes a forum on emerging
technologies and their implications for privacy.

→ PRESERVING EVIDENCE

Then came the case of *Cupp* v. *Murphy* (1973).
In this case, the body of Daniel Murphy's wife
was discovered in their home. She had been stran-
gled, but there was no evidence of a break-in.
Murphy voluntarily went to the police station to
be questioned.

During his interview, police noted a dark spot
on one of Murphy's fingers and residue under his
fingernails. They suspected these were bits of dried
blood from his wife. Police asked Murphy if they

could take scrapings from under his fingernails. He refused, then placed his hands into his pockets.

Police thought Murphy might be cleaning his fingernails and destroying valuable evidence. So they took scrapings even as Murphy protested. Laboratory results confirmed police suspicions. The scrapings held traces of Mrs. Murphy's blood and skin.

Based partly on this evidence, Murphy was convicted of murdering his wife. Murphy appealed his conviction. He said the gathering of evidence from under his fingernails had been a violation of his Fourth Amendment rights. Murphy argued that because the police did not have a warrant, they had no right to take the scrapings.

The Court did not agree. It upheld Murphy's conviction. It said that since Murphy knew he was a suspect, he most likely would have destroyed the evidence as soon as he left the police station. Because the police had no time to get a warrant, they acted properly to preserve the evidence.

Here, then, was another Fourth Amendment precedent. It said that police could act quickly to preserve evidence without a warrant.

The Church Committee

During the 1970s, the Church Committee Report revealed several violations of search and seizure laws committed by the federal government. Various

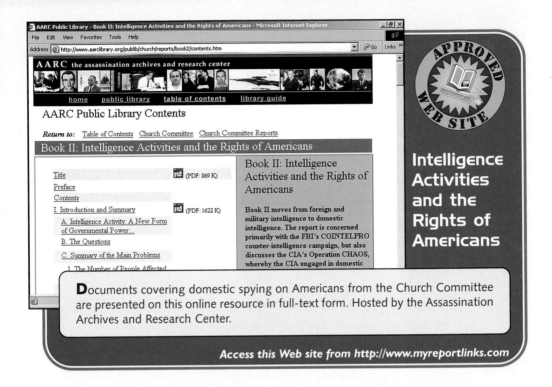

AARC Public Library – Book II: Intelligence Activities and the Rights of Americans - Microsoft Internet Explorer

File   Edit   View   Favorites   Tools   Help

Address http://www.aarclibrary.org/publib/church/reports/book2/contents.htm   Go   Links »

AARC the assassination archives and research center

home   public library   table of contents   library guide

AARC Public Library Contents

Return to: Table of Contents   Church Committee   Church Committee Reports

Book II: Intelligence Activities and the Rights of Americans

Title   (PDF: 869 K)
Preface
Contents
I. Introduction and Summary   (PDF: 1622 K)
   A. Intelligence Activity: A New Form
   of Governmental Power...
   B. The Questions
   C. Summary of the Main Problems
   1. The Number of People Affected

Book II: Intelligence Activities and the Rights of Americans

Book II moves from foreign and military intelligence to domestic intelligence. The report is concerned primarily with the FBI's COINTELPRO counter-intelligence campaign, but also discusses the CIA's Operation CHAOS, whereby the CIA engaged in domestic

Intelligence Activities and the Rights of Americans

Documents covering domestic spying on Americans from the Church Committee are presented on this online resource in full-text form. Hosted by the Assassination Archives and Research Center.

Access this Web site from http://www.myreportlinks.com

agencies had been wiretapping United States citizens and opening their mail without warrants. These agencies claimed to be gathering information in the name of national security.

Many people believed the government's actions were illegal. The agencies, however, argued that because they were protecting national security they did not have to follow search and seizure laws. They believed they could spy on United States citizens without warrants if their work was keeping the nation safe.

But the Church report left many people wondering if anyone should have this power. Could powerful people be trusted to use good judgment without anyone monitoring them? Many people did not think so.

The desire of government agencies to spy without warrants sounded eerily familiar to some people. General surveillance seemed much like the British government's use of writs of assistance.

Yet people also realized that national security was of vital importance. Furthermore, they knew it had to be a secret business. Congress came up with a solution.

THE FOREIGN INTELLIGENCE SURVEILLANCE ACT

Congress passed a new set of laws in 1978. This was called the Foreign Intelligence Surveillance Act (FISA). FISA laws set guidelines for the government to follow when gathering information related to national security.

FISA stated that all surveillance of American citizens needed government approval. However, surveillance related to national security would not go through the regular courts. These requests would go through a special court called the Foreign Intelligence Surveillance Court (FISC). Several judges sat on this court. Any one of them could listen to, and approve or deny, a government request for a warrant.

This system operated in much the same way as the Fourth Amendment system. There were, however, a few important exceptions. First, FISA laws forbid eavesdropping on American citizens except when they were suspected of spying for another country. Next, getting a warrant was easier in a FISA court than in a regular court. FISA requests did not have to meet the standard of probable cause. Finally, hearings for FISA warrants were conducted in secret.

When President Jimmy Carter signed the FISA bill into law on October 25, he added a statement. It said, "The bill requires, for the first time, a prior judicial warrant for all electronic surveillance for foreign intelligence or counterintelligence purposes in the United States in which communications of

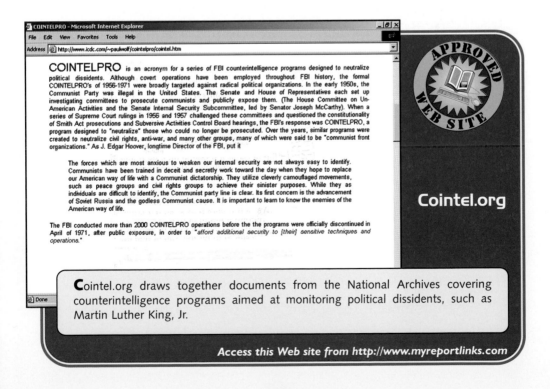

COINTELPRO is an acronym for a series of FBI counterintelligence programs designed to neutralize political dissidents. Although covert operations have been employed throughout FBI history, the formal COINTELPRO's of 1956-1971 were broadly targeted against radical political organizations. In the early 1950s, the Communist Party was illegal in the United States. The Senate and House of Representatives each set up investigating committees to prosecute communists and publicly expose them. (The House Committee on Un-American Activities and the Senate Internal Security Subcommittee, led by Senator Joseph McCarthy). When a series of Supreme Court rulings in 1956 and 1957 challenged these committees and questioned the constitutionality of Smith Act prosecutions and Subversive Activities Control Board hearings, the FBI's response was COINTELPRO, a program designed to "neutralize" those who could no longer be prosecuted. Over the years, similar programs were created to neutralize civil rights, anti-war, and many other groups, many of which were said to be "communist front organizations." As J. Edgar Hoover, longtime Director of the FBI, put it

The forces which are most anxious to weaken our internal security are not always easy to identify. Communists have been trained in deceit and secretly work toward the day when they hope to replace our American way of life with a Communist dictatorship. They utilize cleverly camouflaged movements, such as peace groups and civil rights groups to achieve their sinister purposes. While they as individuals are difficult to identify, the Communist party line is clear. Its first concern is the advancement of Soviet Russia and the godless Communist cause. It is important to learn to know the enemies of the American way of life.

The FBI conducted more than 2000 COINTELPRO operations before the the programs were officially discontinued in April of 1971, after public exposure, in order to "afford additional security to [their] sensitive techniques and operations."

Cointel.org

Cointel.org draws together documents from the National Archives covering counterintelligence programs aimed at monitoring political dissidents, such as Martin Luther King, Jr.

Access this Web site from http://www.myreportlinks.com

U.S. persons might be intercepted."[2] For several decades, FISA laws were an effective way to handle national security.

→CAR SEARCH PROCEDURES

By the 1980s, the Supreme Court realized that procedures for car searches had become somewhat confusing. So it considered a case it hoped would help clarify police procedures.

In *Ross* v. *U.S.* (1982), police stopped Albert Ross based on an informant's tip that he was selling drugs out the trunk of his car. They searched his car and found a gun in the glove compartment and drugs in a brown paper bag in the trunk. Ross was convicted of possession of illegal drugs.

Ross appealed his conviction. He believed that while police had the authority to search his car, they had no authority to open the brown bag. A court of appeals agreed and reversed his conviction. The government then appealed this decision to the Supreme Court. It argued that officers with probable cause had the right to search every part of a car without a warrant.

The Supreme Court agreed. It said that the case of *Carroll* v. *U.S.* (1925) had created an automobile exception to the warrant rule. The automobile exception gave police with probable cause the authority to conduct as thorough a car search without a warrant as they would with one.

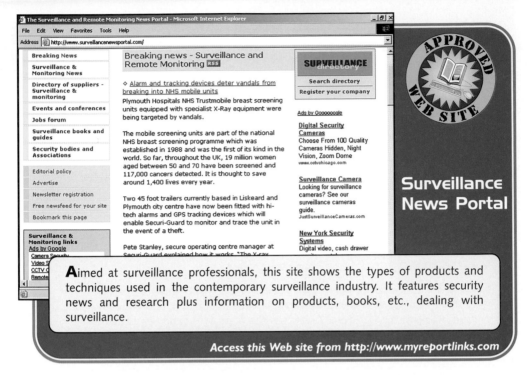

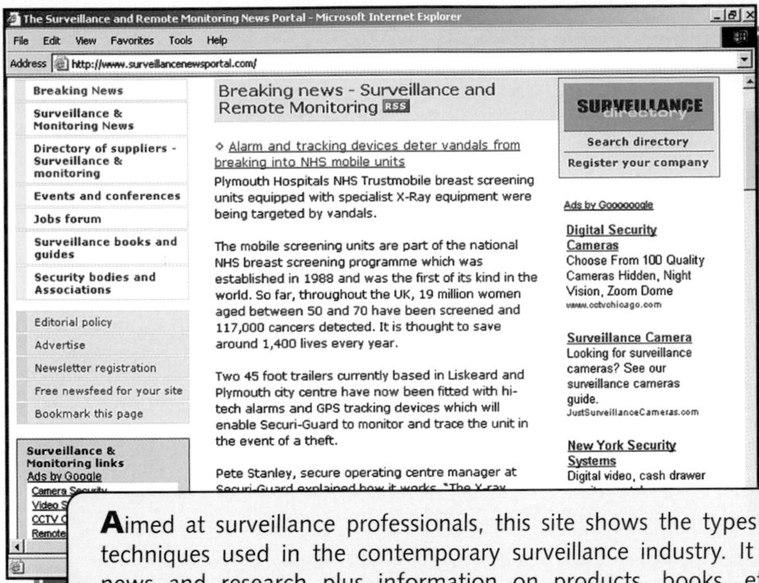
The Surveillance and Remote Monitoring News Portal - Microsoft Internet Explorer
File Edit View Favorites Tools Help
Address http://www.surveillancenewsportal.com/
Breaking News
Surveillance & Monitoring News
Directory of suppliers - Surveillance & monitoring
Events and conferences
Jobs forum
Surveillance books and guides
Security bodies and Associations
Editorial policy
Advertise
Newsletter registration
Free newsfeed for your site
Bookmark this page
Surveillance & Monitoring links
Ads by Google
Breaking news - Surveillance and Remote Monitoring RSS
Alarm and tracking devices deter vandals from breaking into NHS mobile units
Plymouth Hospitals NHS Trustmobile breast screening units equipped with specialist X-Ray equipment were being targeted by vandals.
The mobile screening units are part of the national NHS breast screening programme which was established in 1988 and was the first of its kind in the world. So far, throughout the UK, 19 million women aged between 50 and 70 have been screened and 117,000 cancers detected. It is thought to save around 1,400 lives every year.
Two 45 foot trailers currently based in Liskeard and Plymouth city centre have now been fitted with hi-tech alarms and GPS tracking devices which will enable Securi-Guard to monitor and trace the unit in the event of a theft.
Pete Stanley, secure operating centre manager at
SURVEILLANCE directory
Search directory
Register your company
Ads by Goooooogle
Digital Security Cameras
Choose From 100 Quality Cameras Hidden, Night Vision, Zoom Dome
www.cctvchicago.com
Surveillance Camera
Looking for surveillance cameras? See our surveillance cameras guide.
JustSurveillanceCameras.com
New York Security Systems
Digital video, cash drawer

APPROVED WEB SITE

Surveillance News Portal

Aimed at surveillance professionals, this site shows the types of products and techniques used in the contemporary surveillance industry. It features security news and research plus information on products, books, etc., dealing with surveillance.

Access this Web site from http://www.myreportlinks.com

This meant police could search through every part of a vehicle. They could also search the contents of any containers found in the car. This included backpacks, purses, glove compartments, upholstery, and even the tires themselves.

The Totality of Circumstances

In 1983, the Court dealt again with probable cause. The case of *Illinois* v. *Gates* (1983) began when police in a Chicago suburb received an anonymous letter. It said that a couple in the area was selling drugs.

A detective knew some of the information in the letter was true. He went to a judge to obtain a search warrant for the couple's home. The judge

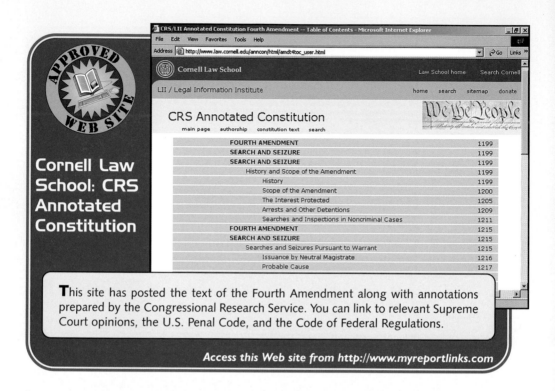

Cornell Law School: CRS Annotated Constitution

This site has posted the text of the Fourth Amendment along with annotations prepared by the Congressional Research Service. You can link to relevant Supreme Court opinions, the U.S. Penal Code, and the Code of Federal Regulations.

Access this Web site from http://www.myreportlinks.com

gave it to him. The police then searched the couple's car. They found 350 pounds of marijuana.

At a pretrial hearing, the Gates's attorney argued that the Exclusionary Rule should apply to the marijuana. He said that the search that found it was based on an improperly issued warrant. The warrant, said the lawyer, had been granted without probable cause according to the standards of the Aguilar-Spinelli test. The judge agreed and the Gates were not convicted.

The state appealed this decision to the Illinois Supreme Court. It upheld the original decision. The state then asked the U.S. Supreme Court to review the case.

The question in this case was whether a search warrant could be issued on the basis of a partially confirmed tip. The Court noted that there was nothing in the informant's letter that showed the author was either honest or that his information was reliable. Therefore, the letter itself did not meet the Aguilar-Spinelli test.

Something more was needed before a judge could find probable cause. The Court decided that the detective's information was just that something. Together, the two rose to the level of probable cause, and the warrant was valid. This case set a new guideline for deciding probable cause. It said that probable cause should not be based on narrowly defined standards. Instead, it should be decided by "the totality of circumstances."

This meant judges needed to consider all of the evidence before them when deciding on probable cause. Their decision had to be based on the whole picture, not just specific pieces of it. This doctrine replaced the Aguilar-Spinelli test.

⮕ U.S. v. LEON

Another Fourth Amendment precedent was set in the case of *U.S. v. Leon* (1984). This case began when a policeman received a tip identifying two people as drug dealers. One was Alberto Leon. Police investigated the tip by watching his home and the cars going to and from it. While on this watch, they noticed that two known drug dealers were regular visitors.

Police took this information to a judge. The judge gave them a warrant to search the cars and the homes they had been watching. The judge based probable cause on the informant's tip, the observations made by the police, and the visits from the known drug dealers to Leon's residence. The police search turned up large quantities of illegal drugs. Four people, including Alberto Leon, were arrested.

At trial, Leon's lawyer argued that there had not been sufficient probable cause for a search warrant to be issued. Therefore, he said, the warrant was invalid. This made the evidence inadmissible.

⊜ In Good Faith

The Court did not address this issue, though. Instead, it looked at how the police had acted while conducting the investigation. The Court decided they had followed correct procedure. They had sought out a warrant before making their search and carried out the search legally. Therefore, the Court said, the police had done nothing wrong. They had acted with the faith that they had been given a good and valid warrant.

The Court went on to say that the Exclusionary Rule is not a right protected by the Constitution. It is a procedure used to encourage proper police behavior. In this case, there had been no improper behavior. The police had acted in good faith. Consequently, the Exclusionary Rule should not be applied. This created a new precedent called "good faith."

THE FOURTH AMENDMENT IN PUBLIC SCHOOLS

In 1985, the Supreme Court ruled on a case involving public school students. In *New Jersey v. T.L.O.* (1985), a fourteen-year-old girl was suspected of smoking cigarettes in the school bathroom. The school principal searched her purse and found marijuana. The girl was convicted in a juvenile court.

The people representing the girl felt that the warrantless search had been a Fourth Amendment violation. They appealed her conviction. The case worked its way to the Supreme Court.

The Court said that school officials were responsible for maintaining a learning environment. This sometimes required relaxing Fourth Amendment procedures. This meant children in public schools had limited privacy rights.

Consequently, the Supreme Court decided that suspicions of wrongdoing by school officials did not have to rise to the level of probable cause. Schools only needed to have a reasonable suspicion that a crime had been committed. Therefore, the Court ruled that the search of the purse had been constitutional.

⊖TECHNOLOGY AND THE FOURTH AMENDMENT

In 1986, Congress passed the Electronic Communications Privacy Act (ECPA). The ECPA was an effort set forth to keep laws current with evolving technology.

In particular, personal computers were becoming widespread. Congress recognized the need to set privacy boundaries regarding the new communication networks it was creating. For example, one

The Electronic Frontier Foundation is a group that seeks to protect free speech, privacy, innovation, and consumer rights in the digital age. Its Web site provides summaries and details of its campaigns and court cases, and links to privacy news stories at other sites.

Access this Web site from http://www.myreportlinks.com

ECPA law said that the government had to have a warrant before surveying e-mail.

➲ PRIVACY FROM THE AIR

The case of *Florida* v. *Riley* (1989) also dealt with the expectation of privacy. This case arose when law enforcement officials received an anonymous tip that marijuana was growing on Michael Riley's property. A police officer investigated, but he could not see into Riley's yard from the street. So he flew a helicopter over the house. From there he was able to look into Riley's greenhouse and observe what he believed to be marijuana. He photographed the greenhouse and took his pictures to a judge. The judge issued a search warrant.

When officers searched Riley's property, they found marijuana growing in his greenhouse. During Riley's trial, though, the Florida court decided that the search warrant had been issued based on improperly obtained evidence. The court did not think the officer should have flown over Riley's house without a warrant. Without the overflight, there would be no evidence to take before a judge to obtain a search warrant. Therefore, there would have been no search. The court ruled that the marijuana could not be used as evidence. Without it, Riley was not convicted.

The state then asked the Florida Supreme Court to review the case. It upheld the first verdict.

This state police officer is monitoring an area from the sky. The 1989 case *Florida v. Riley* set the precedent for law enforcement gathering evidence via flyover.

The state was still not satisfied and so it asked the U.S. Supreme Court to review the case.

The Supreme Court decided that the flight over Riley's house was not a search by Fourth Amendment standards. The Court noted that airplanes and helicopters regularly fly over people's houses. Therefore, people should have no expectation of privacy in items seen from the sky. It ruled that illegal objects visible from the air by the naked eye had no Fourth Amendment protection. This meant the helicopter flight and photo taking needed no warrant.

The Court then said that the photographs rose to the level of probable cause. This made the court's original search warrant valid. The U.S. Supreme Court reversed the ruling.

⇒PRIVACY AND THE SAFETY OF THE PUBLIC

The case of *Skinner* v. *Railway Labor Executives Association* (1989) addressed a different issue. This case involved a policy set by the Federal Railroad Administration (FRA). Upon discovering that alcohol and drugs had led to several train accidents, it allowed railroad companies to conduct drug tests on their employees.

The Railway Labor Executive's Association believed this violated Fourth Amendment rights. It felt that searches that were not based on specific suspicions were unconstitutional. Therefore, unless there was reason to think a person was under the influence of drugs, drug testing was unlawful.

The Supreme Court eventually heard the case. The Court began by saying that the analysis of blood or urine samples was a Fourth Amendment search. Usually, then, it would require a warrant. In this case, though, the Court believed that the government's duty to keep people safe outweighed privacy concerns.

The Court noted that waiting for evidence that a railroad worker was impaired by drugs was not in the interest of public safety. By the time an impaired employee was noticed, it might be too

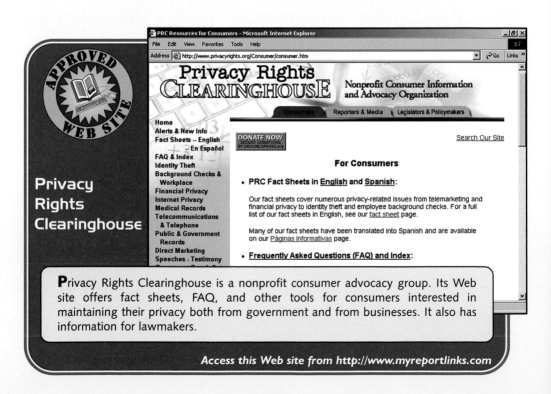

Privacy Rights Clearinghouse

Privacy Rights Clearinghouse is a nonprofit consumer advocacy group. Its Web site offers fact sheets, FAQ, and other tools for consumers interested in maintaining their privacy both from government and from businesses. It also has information for lawmakers.

Access this Web site from http://www.myreportlinks.com

late to prevent an accident. The Court ruled that railroads could order drug tests without suspicions or warrants in the interest of protecting the public.

In 1990, the Court expanded this principle. In *Michigan State Police* v. *Sitz* (1990), the Supreme Court ruled that random roadside checks for drivers under the influence of alcohol or other drugs needed no warrant. They, too, were in the interest of public safety. In its opinion, the Court ruled that the drunken driving problem justified the slight intrusion on citizens.

⇒Drug Testing in the Public Schools

The Court then expanded these safety exceptions to include another group. The ruling in *Vernonia School District* v. *Acton* (1995) added certain public school students to the list of those who could be tested for drugs without a warrant or suspicion.

The case began when school officials started a drug-testing program for students participating in sports. These students were required to have their urine tested at the beginning of a sport season. Then, sometime during the season, a random 10 percent of the team would be tested again.

Urine samples were checked for amphetamines, cocaine, and marijuana. If any of the tests were positive, the student was suspended from play or required to spend six weeks in a drug treatment program with weekly testing. Further

The Supreme Court's decision in Vernonia
School District v. Acton made it legal for
school's to force their student athletes to
submit urine samples for drug tests.

positive tests would result in longer suspensions. None of the tests were conducted with probable cause or a search warrant.

⇒An Issue of Privacy V. Safety

In 1991, seventh-grader James Acton signed up to play football. But his parents refused to sign the consent form that allowed the drug testing. Instead, they filed a lawsuit challenging the drug policy as a violation of their Fourth Amendment rights.

A district court ruled against the Actons. They then appealed. The next court reversed the first decision and ruled for the Actons. Then the school district appealed. The case went to the Supreme Court.

The Court approved of the drug-testing program. In its opinion it said that previous rulings had already approved suspicion-less drug testing in cases involving public safety. In addition, the Court said, *New Jersey* v. *T.L.O.* (1985) had recognized public school students as a group worthy of special protection.

The opinion went on to say, "For their own good and that of their classmates, public school children are routinely required to submit to various physical examinations, and to be vaccinated against various diseases . . ."[3]

Furthermore, the Court said, by joining school teams athletes already subject themselves to additional regulations. They must practice, dress in uniforms, and often follow certain behavior guidelines. The Court saw the drug test as one more requirement for participation.

Therefore, the Court ruled that Vernonia's drug-testing program was not a violation of the Fourth Amendment. The case was remanded to the court of appeals. This decision set the precedent that athletes in public schools could face warrantless drug testing.

6 THE FOURTH AMENDMENT TODAY

O n September 11, 2001, the United States was attacked by a terrorist organization called al-Qaeda. Al-Qaeda flew two airplanes into the World Trade Center in New York City. Another plane was flown into the Pentagon outside of Washington, D.C. A fourth airplane crashed in a field in Pennsylvania while on another mission of destruction. Nearly three thousand Americans were killed in the attacks.

→ THE PATRIOT ACT

One month later, Congress passed a new set of laws called the Patriot Act. The Patriot Act made it easier for the government to investigate United States citizens who might have connections to terrorists.

Many provisions of the Patriot Act related directly to search and seizure issues. For example, the Patriot Act expanded the government's ability to use pen registers. A pen register decodes and records outgoing signals from electronic devices.

Previous laws had allowed the government to install pen registers on telephones. This detected which telephone

USA PATRIOT Act - Microsoft Internet Explorer

File   Edit   View   Favorites   Tools   Help

Address   http://www.whitehouse.gov/infocus/patriotact/

○ Health Care
○ Homeland Security
○ Hurricanes
○ Immigration
○ Jobs & Economy
○ Judicial Nominations
○ Medicare
○ Middle East
○ National Security
○ Pandemic Flu
○ Patriot Act
○ Renewal in Iraq
○ Social Security

More Issues →

News

○ Current News
○ Press Briefings
○ Proclamations
○ Executive Orders
○ Radio

RSS RSS Feeds

Major Speeches

○ Press Conference
○ Secure Fence Act
○ Military Co...
○ Safe Port...
○ School S...

Done

USA PATRIOT Act

USA PATRIOT Act

PROTECTING THE HOMELAND

President George W. Bush is joined by House and Senate representatives as he signs H.R. 3199, USA Patriot Improvement and Reauthorization Act of 2005, Thursday, March 9, 2006 in the East Room of the White House. From left to right are U.S. Sen. Jim Talent, R-Mo.; U.S. Sen. Pat Roberts, R-Kan.;

IN FOCUS

◇ **SPEECHES & NEWS RELEASES**

March 9, 2006
President Signs USA PATRIOT Improvement and Reauthorization Act

Fact Sheet: Safeguarding America: President Bush Signs Patriot Act Reauthorization

President's Statement on H.R. 199, the "USA PATRIOT Improvement and Reauthorization Act"

President Sig...
2271

March 2, 20...
President A...
to Renew P...

APPROVED WEB SITE

The White House: USA PATRIOT Act page provides the Bush administration's perspective on the value of the USA Patriot Act. There is a description of its use in legal cases in which it is said to have come into play.

numbers criminals were calling. The Patriot Act extended this to include all electronic communications including the Internet. Now the government could track a person's e-mail and Web-surfing activities.

In addition, the Patriot Act gave the government the authority to conduct "roving wiretaps." These investigations allowed electronic surveillance on any communication device a suspect was using. With one general permit, the government could now track a person's communication whether by land phone, cell phone, or e-mail.

Finally, the law allowed the government access to the books, records, and documents of suspects. This included medical information, educational files, business and bank records, and even library accounts.

Many of these new provisions fell under FISA laws. Therefore, the government did not need a warrant from a regular court to conduct terrorist-related searches. It would obtain its permission from a FISA court.

In many instances, the Patriot Act made obtaining FISA permission easier. Now FISA courts did not always require evidence to meet the standard of probable cause. Instead, the government only

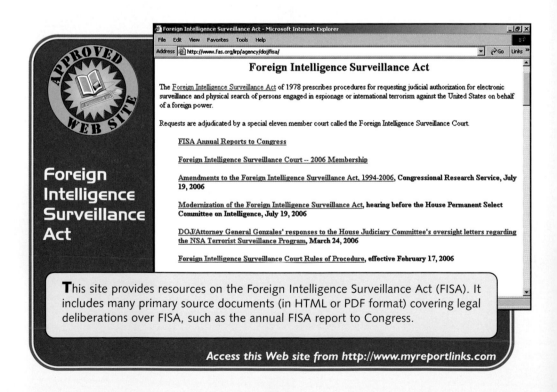

APPROVED WEB SITE

Foreign Intelligence Surveillance Act

Foreign Intelligence Surveillance Act - Microsoft Internet Explorer

File Edit View Favorites Tools Help

Address http://www.fas.org/irp/agency/doj/fisa/

Foreign Intelligence Surveillance Act

The Foreign Intelligence Surveillance Act of 1978 prescribes procedures for requesting judicial authorization for electronic surveillance and physical search of persons engaged in espionage or international terrorism against the United States on behalf of a foreign power.

Requests are adjudicated by a special eleven member court called the Foreign Intelligence Surveillance Court.

FISA Annual Reports to Congress

Foreign Intelligence Surveillance Court -- 2006 Membership

Amendments to the Foreign Intelligence Surveillance Act, 1994-2006, **Congressional Research Service, July 19, 2006**

Modernization of the Foreign Intelligence Surveillance Act, **hearing before the House Permanent Select Committee on Intelligence, July 19, 2006**

DOJ/Attorney General Gonzales' responses to the House Judiciary Committee's oversight letters regarding the NSA Terrorist Surveillance Program, **March 24, 2006**

Foreign Intelligence Surveillance Court Rules of Procedure, **effective February 17, 2006**

This site provides resources on the Foreign Intelligence Surveillance Act (FISA). It includes many primary source documents (in HTML or PDF format) covering legal deliberations over FISA, such as the annual FISA report to Congress.

Access this Web site from http://www.myreportlinks.com

needed to say that the requested information was related to a terrorist investigation.[1]

⮕ THE NSA PROGRAM

In December 2005, the American public learned of another surveillance program designed to fight terrorists. According to an article in *The New York Times,* President George W. Bush had authorized the National Security Agency (NSA) to eavesdrop on persons suspected of terrorist activities. It had been in effect since 2002.

This program listened in on phone calls between people in the United States and another country when one of the parties was suspected of being a terrorist. The program became known as the NSA surveillance program.

The NSA program did not require warrants from a regular court. This was because it dealt with national security. However, the program did not seek permission from FISA courts, either. This meant the government was conducting surveillance with no one to oversee its actions.

⮕ THE NSA PROGRAM AND THE LAW

Many people were outraged when they learned of the program. They believed that by ignoring FISA regulations, the NSA program violated the law.

President Bush responded by saying that the NSA program was necessary to protect the American people. The program was not monitoring the calls of all Americans. It was only monitoring calls between someone in the United States and someone in another country thought to be connected with terrorism. The president went on to say that the terrorists "attacked us before; they will attack us again if they can, and we're going to do everything we can to stop them."[2]

President Bush felt the NSA program was both legal and justified. He believed that Congress had given him permission to create programs like this

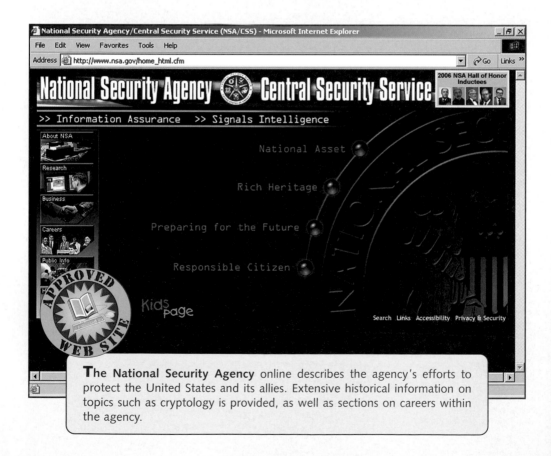

The National Security Agency online describes the agency's efforts to protect the United States and its allies. Extensive historical information on topics such as cryptology is provided, as well as sections on careers within the agency.

when it approved the Authority for Use of Military Force. This law had been passed one week after the September 11 attacks. It said that ". . . the President is authorized to use all necessary and appropriate force against those nations, organizations, or persons he determines planned, authorized, committed or aided the terrorist attacks that occurred on September 11, 2001."[3]

➡THE NSA PROGRAM IS QUESTIONED

Alberto Gonzales was the United States' attorney general at the time. The attorney general is the chief legal advisor for the executive branch of the government. He, too, believed the program was entirely legal. In a January 2006 speech, he said, ". . . the Constitution gives the President all authority necessary . . ." to protect the safety of all Americans.[4]

Others were not so sure. Many people did not believe that either the authorization of military force or the Constitution gave the president the power to ignore the Fourth Amendment or FISA laws.

America's largest law association, the American Bar Association (ABA), put together a task force to study the NSA program. Its study concluded that ". . . any electronic surveillance inside the United States by any U.S. government agency for foreign intelligence purposes must comply with the provisions of FISA . . ."[5]

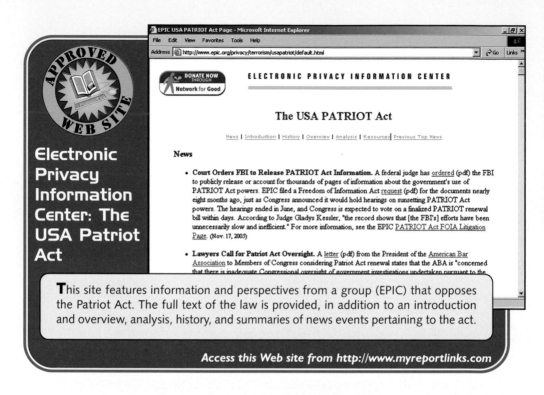

EPIC USA PATRIOT Act Page - Microsoft Internet Explorer

File   Edit   View   Favorites   Tools   Help

Address   http://www.epic.org/privacy/terrorism/usapatriot/default.html   Go   Links »

ELECTRONIC PRIVACY INFORMATION CENTER

DONATE NOW THROUGH Network for Good

The USA PATRIOT Act

News | Introduction | History | Overview | Analysis | Resources | Previous Top News

News

- **Court Orders FBI to Release PATRIOT Act Information.** A federal judge has ordered (pdf) the FBI to publicly release or account for thousands of pages of information about the government's use of PATRIOT Act powers. EPIC filed a Freedom of Information Act request (pdf) for the documents nearly eight months ago, just as Congress announced it would hold hearings on sunsetting PATRIOT Act powers. The hearings ended in June, and Congress is expected to vote on a finalized PATRIOT renewal bill within days. According to Judge Gladys Kessler, "the record shows that [the FBI's] efforts have been unnecessarily slow and inefficient." For more information, see the EPIC PATRIOT Act FOIA Litigation Page. (Nov. 17, 2005)

- **Lawyers Call for Patriot Act Oversight.** A letter (pdf) from the President of the American Bar Association to Members of Congress considering Patriot Act renewal states that the ABA is "concerned that there is inadequate Congressional oversight of government investigations undertaken pursuant to the

Electronic Privacy Information Center: The USA Patriot Act

This site features information and perspectives from a group (EPIC) that opposes the Patriot Act. The full text of the law is provided, in addition to an introduction and overview, analysis, history, and summaries of news events pertaining to the act.

Access this Web site from http://www.myreportlinks.com

➔THE NSA PROGRAM AND FISA

Some people wondered why the president felt he needed to go around FISA laws. The Patriot Act had increased the number of judges on the FISA court. It had expanded the definition of who could be surveilled. It had relaxed the requirements for obtaining surveillance permission.

Furthermore, FISA had been amended to help the government deal with emergency situations. When it was first passed, FISA gave the government permission to conduct electronic surveillances in emergency situations without approval from the FISA court. Then, within twenty-four hours, the government could go to the court and seek approval for its actions. New laws extended this window to seventy-two hours. Now a warrant could be obtained three days after any eavesdropping was done.

Many people argued that with all of the FISA expansions, the laws were adequate in dealing with terrorists. If they were not, the president needed to ask Congress to make changes in the law.

Yet President Bush maintained that FISA did not give security agencies enough tools to deal with terrorists in an age of sophisticated technology. He believed that national security agencies needed unrestricted leeway in its search procedures.[6]

Opponents believed that the government was once again using unlimited search powers. They worried that in this general approach to surveillance, the privacy of law-abiding citizens would be violated. Past history showed that unchecked power often led to abuse.

LAWSUITS AND THE NSA PROGRAM

It was not long before groups were filing lawsuits against the program. By 2006, several civil liberties groups had gone to court asking judges to stop the program on the grounds that it was unconstitutional.

President Bush, however, wanted these lawsuits dropped in the name of national security. He believed that the legality of the NSA program

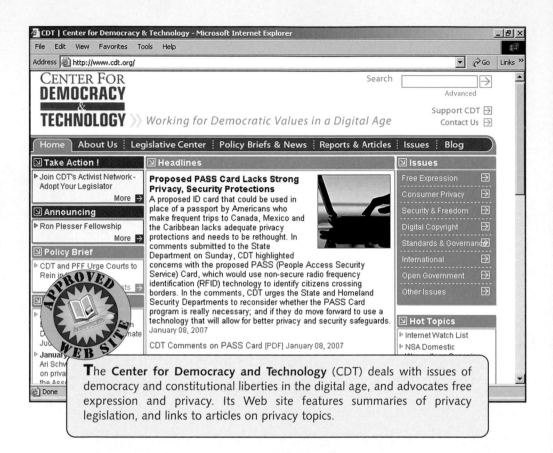

CDT | Center for Democracy & Technology - Microsoft Internet Explorer

File   Edit   View   Favorites   Tools   Help

Address http://www.cdt.org/

CENTER FOR
DEMOCRACY
&
TECHNOLOGY >> *Working for Democratic Values in a Digital Age*

Search

Advanced

Support CDT
Contact Us

Home   About Us   Legislative Center   Policy Briefs & News   Reports & Articles   Issues   Blog

Take Action !
Join CDT's Activist Network -
Adopt Your Legislator
More

Announcing
Ron Plesser Fellowship
More

Policy Brief
CDT and PFF Urge Courts to
Rein in

Headlines
**Proposed PASS Card Lacks Strong
Privacy, Security Protections**
A proposed ID card that could be used in
place of a passport by Americans who
make frequent trips to Canada, Mexico and
the Caribbean lacks adequate privacy
protections and needs to be rethought. In
comments submitted to the State
Department on Sunday, CDT highlighted
concerns with the proposed PASS (People Access Security
Service) Card, which would use non-secure radio frequency
identification (RFID) technology to identify citizens crossing
borders. In the comments, CDT urges the State and Homeland
Security Departments to reconsider whether the PASS Card
program is really necessary; and if they do move forward to use a
technology that will allow for better privacy and security safeguards.
January 08, 2007

CDT Comments on PASS Card [PDF] January 08, 2007

Issues
Free Expression
Consumer Privacy
Security & Freedom
Digital Copyright
Standards & Governance
International
Open Government
Other Issues

Hot Topics
Internet Watch List
NSA Domestic

The **Center for Democracy and Technology** (CDT) deals with issues of democracy and constitutional liberties in the digital age, and advocates free expression and privacy. Its Web site features summaries of privacy legislation, and links to articles on privacy topics.

could not be determined without giving away
secret information that would help terrorists.[7]

DATA MINING

Many people saw the NSA surveillance as an
unconstitutional data-mining program. Data mining
is the process of searching large volumes of data
for specific information. It uses complex computer
programs that sift through huge amounts of information looking for specific words and even ideas.
It then looks for patterns in their usage. This

process can provide information about a person's associates and activities.

In June 2006, the public learned that the government had been using another data-mining program to catch terrorists. This one searched through bank records.

The CIA and FBI had been analyzing information from a company that monitored financial transactions all over the world. Many of the transactions were made in foreign countries. But officials also looked at the business records of individuals, businesses, and charities in the United States. The program had been able to identify some terrorists and groups that were helping them. Yet people wondered if this program also violated FISA laws.

Data mining by the federal government for national security alerted the public to new threats to their privacy. What protections did the Fourth Amendment provide in the "information age"? Were people protected from data mining done by law enforcement officials in the name of criminal investigations?

⊖THE FOURTH AMENDMENT AND TWENTY-FIRST CENTURY TECHNOLOGY

Data mining was not the only technology that opened new questions about the Fourth Amendment. For example, electronic listening devices

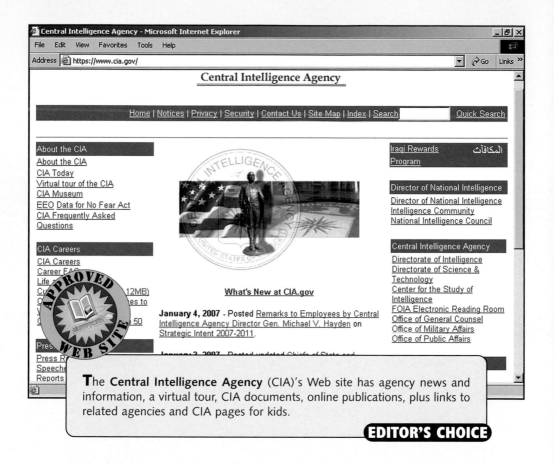

Central Intelligence Agency - Microsoft Internet Explorer

File   Edit   View   Favorites   Tools   Help

Address https://www.cia.gov/   Go   Links »

Central Intelligence Agency

Home | Notices | Privacy | Security | Contact Us | Site Map | Index | Search   Quick Search

About the CIA
About the CIA
CIA Today
Virtual tour of the CIA
CIA Museum
EEO Data for No Fear Act
CIA Frequently Asked
Questions

CIA Careers
CIA Careers
Career FAQ
Life A
Cu   (12MB)
C   es to
V
C   50

Pres
Press R
Speeche
Reports

Iraqi Rewards   المكافآت
Program

Director of National Intelligence
Director of National Intelligence
Intelligence Community
National Intelligence Council

Central Intelligence Agency
Directorate of Intelligence
Directorate of Science &
Technology
Center for the Study of
Intelligence
FOIA Electronic Reading Room
Office of General Counsel
Office of Military Affairs
Office of Public Affairs

What's New at CIA.gov

January 4, 2007 - Posted Remarks to Employees by Central
Intelligence Agency Director Gen. Michael V. Hayden on
Strategic Intent 2007-2011.

The **Central Intelligence Agency** (CIA)'s Web site has agency news and
information, a virtual tour, CIA documents, online publications, plus links to
related agencies and CIA pages for kids.

EDITOR'S CHOICE

have become so small they can be hidden in calculators or pens.

Laser technology has also invented supersecret eavesdropping devices. One tool shoots a laser beam at an object near the person who is being monitored. The device detects the sound waves against the object. It then translates the waves into the words the person is saying. This allows authorities to eavesdrop from far away.

The Global Positioning System (GPS) is another technology that can be used for surveillance. GPS is a satellite navigation system. It consists of many satellites that broadcast signals to the earth from space. Special receivers on the ground pick up these signals. They then translate and transmit the information to a computer or special tracking device. GPS is used for navigation, mapmaking, land surveying, and scientific research.

It can also be used in law enforcement. For example, GPS tracking devices can be hidden in a vehicle, and the vehicle can be tracked.

All of these new technologies present Fourth Amendment issues. Is listening in on a conversation with a laser tool a search? What about tracking a suspect with a GPS system? Future Supreme Court cases will have to determine the boundaries of these sorts of searches.

IMMIGRATION AND THE FOURTH AMENDMENT

Another current Fourth Amendment issue involves immigration. Regulating the people who come into the United States protects the American public. The United States does not want to admit terrorists or criminals into the country. Nor does it want to admit drugs or weapons.

Unwarranted searches have always been allowed at the border. They are thought of as the nation's right to protect itself. Many of the places where people enter the United States from

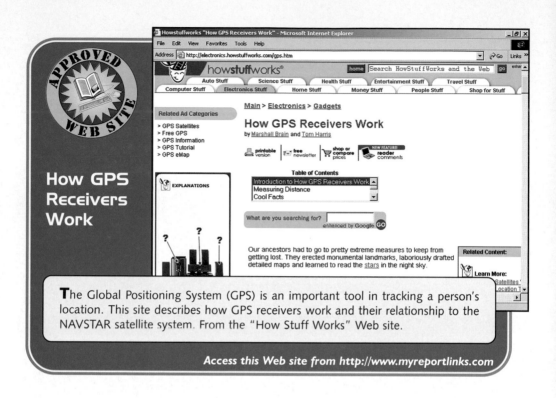

How GPS Receivers Work

The Global Positioning System (GPS) is an important tool in tracking a person's location. This site describes how GPS receivers work and their relationship to the NAVSTAR satellite system. From the "How Stuff Works" Web site.

Access this Web site from http://www.myreportlinks.com

another country have customs checks. These are places where officials check the legal papers of those coming into the country. Officials might also search people for illegal substances.

Customs officials need no warrant, no probable cause, or even suspicion to search people or vehicles at the border. Therefore, the United States government wants to strengthen its border checks to help protect the nation.

⊖THE FOURTH AMENDMENT TOMORROW

The nation's founders could never have anticipated there could be laser beams that would capture conversations from two hundred feet away. They could not have predicted a system of satellites circling Earth and sending information to small receivers on the ground.

They, did, however, know what privacy was. They also knew it was a right they wanted to protect. By carefully crafting the Fourth Amendment, they ensured this right to generations of Americans yet to come.

The Constitution of the United States

The text of the Constitution is presented here. All words are given their modern spelling and capitalization. Brackets [ ] indicate parts that have been changed or set aside by amendments.

Preamble

We the People of the United States, in Order to form a more perfect Union, establish Justice, insure domestic Tranquillity, provide for the common defence, promote the general Welfare, and secure the Blessings of Liberty to ourselves and our Posterity, do ordain and establish this Constitution for the United States of America.

Article I
The Legislative Branch

Section 1. All legislative powers herein granted shall be vested in a Congress of the United States, which shall consist of a Senate and House of Representatives.

The House of Representatives

Section 2. The House of Representatives shall be composed of members chosen every second year by the people of the several states, and the electors in each state shall have the qualifications requisite for electors of the most numerous branch of the state legislature.

No person shall be a Representative who shall not have attained to the age of twenty five years, and been seven years a citizen of the United States, and who shall not, when elected, be an inhabitant of that state in which he shall be chosen.

Representatives and direct taxes shall be apportioned among the several states which may be included within this union, according to their respective numbers, [which shall be determined by adding to the whole number of free persons, including those bound to service for a term of years, and excluding Indians not taxed, three fifths of all other persons]. The actual Enumeration shall be made within three years after the first meeting of the Congress of the United States, and within every subsequent term of ten years, in such manner as they shall by law direct. The number of Representatives shall not exceed one for every thirty thousand, but each state shall have at least one Representative; [and until such enumeration shall be made, the state of New Hampshire shall be entitled to chuse three, Massachusetts eight, Rhode Island and Providence Plantations one, Connecticut five, New York six, New Jersey four, Pennsylvania eight, Delaware one, Maryland six, Virginia ten, North Carolina five, South Carolina five, and Georgia three].

When vacancies happen in the Representation from any state, the executive authority thereof shall issue writs of election to fill such vacancies.

The House of Representatives shall choose their speaker and other officers; and shall have the sole power of impeachment.

The Senate

Section 3. The Senate of the United States shall be composed of two Senators from each state, [chosen by the legislature thereof,] for six years; and each Senator shall have one vote.

Immediately after they shall be assembled in consequence of the first election, they shall be divided as equally as may be into three classes. The seats of the Senators of the first class shall be vacated at the expiration of the second year, of the second class at the expiration of the fourth year, and the third class at the expiration of the sixth year, so that one third may be chosen every second year; [and if vacancies happen by resignation, or otherwise, during the recess of the legislature of any state, the executive thereof may make temporary appointments until the next meeting of the legislature, which shall then fill such vacancies].

No person shall be a Senator who shall not have attained to the age of thirty years, and been nine years a citizen of the United States and who shall not, when elected, be an inhabitant of that state for which he shall be chosen.

The Vice President of the United States shall be President of the Senate, but shall have no vote, unless they be equally divided.

The Senate shall choose their other officers, and also a President pro tempore, in the absence of the Vice President, or when he shall exercise the office of President of the United States.

The Senate shall have the sole power to try all impeachments. When sitting for that purpose, they shall be on oath or affirmation. When the President of the United States is tried, the Chief Justice shall preside: And no person shall be convicted without the concurrence of two thirds of the members present.

Judgment in cases of impeachment shall not extend further than to removal from office, and disqualification to hold and enjoy any office of honor, trust or profit under the United States: but the party convicted shall nevertheless be liable and subject to indictment, trial, judgment and punishment, according to law.

Organization of Congress

Section 4. The times, places and manner of holding elections for Senators and Representatives, shall be prescribed in each state by the legislature thereof; but the Congress may at any time by law make or alter such regulations, [except as to the places of choosing senators].

The Congress shall assemble at least once in every year, [and such meeting shall be on the first Monday in December], unless they shall by law appoint a different day.

Section 5. Each House shall be the judge of the elections, returns and qualifications of its own members, and a majority of each shall constitute a quorum to do business; but a smaller number may adjourn from day to day, and may be authorized to compel the attendance of absent members, in such manner, and under such penalties as each House may provide.

Each House may determine the rules of its proceedings, punish its members for disorderly behavior, and, with the concurrence of two thirds, expel a member.

Each House shall keep a journal of its proceedings, and from time to time publish the same, excepting such parts as may in their judgment require secrecy; and the yeas and nays of the members of either House on any question shall, at the desire of one fifth of those present, be entered on the journal.

Neither House, during the session of Congress, shall, without the consent of the other, adjourn for more than three days, nor to any other place than that in which the two Houses shall be sitting.

Section 6. The Senators and Representatives shall receive a compensation for their services, to be ascertained by law, and paid out of the treasury of the United States. They shall in all cases, except treason, felony and breach of the peace, be privileged from arrest during their attendance at the session of their respective Houses, and in going to and returning from the same; and for any speech or debate in either House, they shall not be questioned in any other place.

No Senator or Representative shall, during the time for which he was elected, be appointed to any civil office under the authority of the United States, which shall have been created, or the emoluments whereof shall have been increased during such time: and no person holding any office under the United States, shall be a member of either House during his continuance in office.

Section 7. All bills for raising revenue shall originate in the House of Representatives; but the Senate may propose or concur with amendments as on other Bills.

Every bill which shall have passed the House of Representatives and the Senate, shall, before it become a law, be presented to the President of the United States; if he approve he shall sign it, but if not he shall return it, with his objections to that House in which it shall have originated, who shall enter the objections at large on their journal, and proceed to reconsider it. If after such reconsideration two thirds of that House shall agree to pass the bill, it shall be sent, together with the objections, to the other House, by which it shall likewise be reconsidered, and if approved by two thirds of that House, it shall become a law. But in all such cases the votes of both Houses shall be determined by yeas and nays, and the names of the persons voting for and against the bill shall be entered on the journal of each House respectively. If any bill shall not be returned by the President within ten days (Sundays excepted) after it shall have been presented to him, the same shall be a law, in like manner as if he had signed it, unless the Congress by their adjournment prevent its return, in which case it shall not be a law.

Every order, resolution, or vote to which the concurrence of the Senate and House of Representatives may be necessary (except on a question of adjournment) shall be presented to the President of the United States; and before the same shall take effect, shall be approved by him, or being disapproved by him, shall be repassed by two thirds of the Senate and House of Representatives, according to the rules and limitations prescribed in the case of a bill.

Powers Granted to Congress
The Congress shall have the power:

Section 8. To lay and collect taxes, duties, imposts and excises, to pay the debts and provide for the common defense and general welfare of the United States; but all duties, imposts and excises shall be uniform throughout the United States;

To borrow money on the credit of the United States;

To regulate commerce with foreign nations, and among the several states, and with the Indian tribes;

To establish a uniform rule of naturalization, and uniform laws on the subject of bankruptcies throughout the United States;

To coin money, regulate the value thereof, and of foreign coin, and fix the standard of weights and measures;

To provide for the punishment of counterfeiting the securities and current coin of the United States;

To establish post offices and post roads;

To promote the progress of science and useful arts, by securing for limited times to authors and inventors the exclusive right to their respective writings and discoveries;

To constitute tribunals inferior to the Supreme Court;

To define and punish piracies and felonies committed on the high seas, and offenses against the law of nations;

To declare war, grant letters of marque and reprisal, and make rules concerning captures on land and water;

To raise and support armies, but no appropriation of money to that use shall be for a longer term than two years;

To provide and maintain a navy;

To make rules for the government and regulation of the land and naval forces;

To provide for calling forth the militia to execute the laws of the union, suppress insurrections and repel invasions;

To provide for organizing, arming, and disciplining, the militia, and for governing such part of them as may be employed in the service of the United States, reserving to the states respectively, the appointment of the officers, and the authority of training the militia according to the discipline prescribed by Congress;

To exercise exclusive legislation in all cases whatsoever, over such District (not exceeding ten miles square) as may, by cession of particular states, and the acceptance of Congress, become the seat of the government of the United States, and to exercise like authority over all places purchased by the consent of the legislature of the state in which the same shall be, for the erection of forts, magazines, arsenals, dockyards, and other needful buildings;—And

To make all laws which shall be necessary and proper for carrying into execution the foregoing powers, and all other powers vested by this Constitution in the government of the United States, or in any depart-ment or officer thereof.

Powers Forbidden to Congress

Section 9. The migration or importation of such persons as any of the states now existing shall think proper to admit, shall not be prohibited by the Congress prior to the year one thousand eight hundred and eight, but a tax or duty may be imposed on such importation, not exceeding ten dollars for each person.

The privilege of the writ of habeas corpus shall not be suspended, unless when in cases of rebellion or invasion the public safety may require it.

No bill of attainder or ex post facto law shall be passed.

No capitation, [or other direct,] tax shall be laid, unless in proportion to the census or enumeration herein before directed to be taken.

No tax or duty shall be laid on articles exported from any state.

No preference shall be given by any regulation of commerce or revenue to the ports of one state over those of another: nor shall vessels bound to, or from, one state, be obliged to enter, clear or pay duties in another.

No money shall be drawn from the treasury, but in consequence of appropriations made by law; and a regular statement and account of receipts and expenditures of all public money shall be published from time to time.

No title of nobility shall be granted by the United States: and no person holding any office of profit or trust under them, shall, without the consent of the Congress, accept of any present, emolument, office, or title, of any kind whatever, from any king, prince, or foreign state.

Powers Forbidden to the States

Section 10. No state shall enter into any treaty, alliance, or confederation; grant letters of marque and reprisal; coin money; emit bills of credit; make anything but gold and silver coin a tender in payment of debts; pass any bill of attainder, ex post facto law, or law impairing the obligation of contracts, or grant any title of nobility.

No state shall, without the consent of the Congress, lay any imposts or duties on imports or exports, except what may be absolutely necessary for executing its inspection laws: and the net produce of all duties and imposts, laid by any state on imports or exports, shall be for the use of the treasury of the United States; and all such laws shall be subject to the revision and control of the Congress.

No state shall, without the consent of Congress, lay any duty of tonnage, keep troops, or ships of war in time of peace, enter into any agreement or compact with another state, or with a foreign power, or engage in war, unless actually invaded, or in such imminent danger as will not admit of delay.

Article II
The Executive Branch

Section 1. The executive power shall be vested in a President of the United States of America. He shall hold his office during the term of four years, and, together with the Vice President, chosen for the same term, be elected, as follows:

Each state shall appoint, in such manner as the legislature thereof may direct, a number of electors, equal to the whole number of Senators and Representatives to which the State may be entitled in the Congress: but no Senator or Representative, or person holding an office of trust or profit under the United States, shall be appointed an elector.

[The electors shall meet in their respective states, and vote by ballot for two persons, of whom one at least shall not be an inhabitant of the same state with themselves. And they shall make a list of all the persons voted for, and of the number of votes for each; which list they shall sign and certify, and transmit sealed to the seat of the government of the United States, directed to the President of the Senate. The President of the Senate shall, in the presence of the Senate and House of Representatives, open all the certificates, and the votes shall then be counted. The person having the greatest number of votes shall be the President, if such number be a majority of the whole number of electors appointed; and if there be more than one who have such majority, and have an equal number of votes, then the House of Representatives shall immediately choose by ballot one of them for President; and if no person have a majority, then from the five highest on the list the said House shall in like manner choose the President. But in choosing the President, the votes shall be taken by States, the representation from each state having one vote; A quorum for this purpose shall consist of a member or members from two thirds of the states, and a majority of all the states shall be necessary to a choice. In every case, after the choice of the President, the person having the greatest number of votes of the electors shall be the Vice President. But if there should remain two or more who have equal votes, the Senate shall choose from them by ballot the Vice President.]

The Congress may determine the time of choosing the electors, and the day on which they shall give their votes; which day shall be the same throughout the United States.

No person except a natural born citizen, or a citizen of the United States, at the time of the adoption of this Constitution, shall be eligible to the office of President; neither shall any person be eligible to that office who shall not have attained to the age of thirty-five years, and been fourteen Years a resident within the United States.

In case of the removal of the President from office, or of his death, resignation, or inability to discharge the powers and duties of the said office, the same shall devolve on the Vice President, and the Congress may by law provide for the case of removal, death, resignation or inability, both of the President and Vice President, declaring what officer shall then act as President, and such officer shall act accordingly, until the disability be removed, or a President shall be elected.

The President shall, at stated times, receive for his services, a compensation, which shall neither be increased nor diminished during the period for which he shall have been elected, and he shall not receive within that period any other emolument from the United States, or any of them.

Before he enter on the execution of his office, he shall take the following oath or affirmation:—"I do solemnly swear (or affirm) that I will faithfully execute the office of President of the United States, and will to the best of my ability, preserve, protect and defend the Constitution of the United States."

Section 2. The President shall be commander-in-chief of the Army and Navy of the United States, and of the militia of the several states, when called into the actual service of the United States; he may require the opinion, in writing, of the principal officer in each of the executive departments, upon any subject relating to the duties of their respective offices, and he shall have power to grant reprieves and pardons for offenses against the United States, except in cases of impeachment.

He shall have power, by and with the advice and consent of the Senate, to make treaties, provided two-thirds of the Senators present concur; and he shall nominate, and by and with the advice and consent of the Senate, shall appoint ambassadors, other public ministers and consuls, judges of the Supreme Court, and all other officers of the United States, whose appointments are not herein otherwise provided for, and which shall be established by law: but the Congress may by law vest the appointment of such inferior officers, as they think proper, in the President alone, in the courts of law, or in the heads of departments.

The President shall have power to fill up all vacancies that may happen during the recess of the Senate, by granting commissions which shall expire at the end of their next session.

Section 3. He shall from time to time give to the Congress information of the state of the union, and recommend to their consideration such measures as he shall judge necessary and expedient; he may, on extraordinary occasions, convene both Houses, or either of them, and in case of disagreement between them, with respect to the time of adjournment, he may adjourn them to such time as he shall think proper; he shall receive ambassadors and other public ministers; he shall take care that the laws be faithfully executed, and shall commission all the officers of the United States.

Section 4. The President, Vice President and all civil officers of the United States, shall be removed from office on impeachment for, and conviction of, treason, bribery, or other high crimes and misdemeanors.

Article III
The Judicial Branch

Section 1. The judicial power of the United States, shall be vested in one Supreme Court, and in such inferior courts as the Congress may from time to time ordain and establish. The judges, both of the supreme and inferior courts, shall hold their offices during good behaviour, and shall, at stated times, receive for their services, a compensation, which shall not be diminished during their continuance in office.

Section 2. The judicial power shall extend to all cases, in law and equity, arising under this Constitution, the laws of the United States, and treaties made, or which shall be made, under their authority;—to all cases affecting ambassadors, other public ministers and consuls;—to all cases of admiralty and maritime jurisdiction, [—to controversies to which the United States shall be a party;—to controversies between two or more states, [between a state and citizens of another state;], between citizens of different states;—between citizens of the same state, claiming lands under grants of different states, and between a state, or the citizens thereof, and foreign states, [citizens or subjects].

In all cases affecting ambassadors, other public ministers and consuls, and those in which a state shall be party, the Supreme Court shall have original jurisdiction. In all the other cases before mentioned, the Supreme Court shall have appellate jurisdiction, both as to law and fact, with such exceptions, and under such regulations as the Congress shall make.

The trial of all crimes, except in cases of impeach-ment, shall be by jury; and such trial shall be held in the state where the said crimes shall have been committed; but when not committed within any state, the trial shall be at such place or places as the Congress may by law have directed.

Section 3. Treason against the United States, shall consist only in levying war against them, or in adhering to their enemies, giving them aid and comfort. No person shall be convicted of treason unless on the testimony of two witnesses to the same overt act, or on confession in open court.

The Congress shall have power to declare the punishment of treason, but no attainder of treason shall work corruption of blood, or forfeiture except during the life of the person attainted.

Article IV
Relation of the States to Each Other

Section 1. Full faith and credit shall be given in each state to the public acts, records, and judicial proceedings of every other state. And the Congress may by general laws prescribe the manner in which such acts, records, and proceedings shall be proved, and the effect thereof.

Section 2. The citizens of each state shall be entitled to all privileges and immunities of citizens in the several states.

A person charged in any state with treason, felony, or other crime, who shall flee from justice, and be found in another state, shall on demand of the executive authority of the state from which he fled, be delivered up, to be removed to the state having jurisdiction of the crime.

[No person held to service or labor in one state, under the laws thereof, escaping into another, shall, in consequence of any law or regulation therein, be discharged from such service or labor, but shall be delivered up on claim of the party to whom such service or labor may be due.]

Federal-State Relations

Section 3. New states may be admitted by the Congress into this Union; but no new states shall be formed or erected within the jurisdiction of any other state, nor any state be formed by the junction of two or more states, without the consent of the legislatures of the states concerned, as well as of the Congress.

The Congress shall have power to dispose of and make all needful rules and regulations respecting the territory or other property belonging to the United States; and nothing in this Constitution shall be so construed as to prejudice any claims of the United States, or of any particular state.

Section 4. The United States shall guarantee to every state in this union a republican form of government, and shall protect each of them against invasion; and on application of the legislature, or of the executive (when the legislature cannot be convened) against domestic violence.

Article V
Amending the Constitution

The Congress, whenever two thirds of both houses shall deem it necessary, shall propose amendments to this Constitution, or, on the application of the legislatures of two thirds of the several states, shall call a convention for proposing amendments, which, in either case, shall be valid to all intents and purposes, as part of this Constitution, when ratified by the legislatures of three fourths of the several states, or by conventions in three fourths thereof, as the one or the other mode of ratification may be proposed by the Congress; provided [that no amendment which may be made prior to the year one thousand eight hundred and eight shall in any manner affect the first and fourth clauses in the ninth section of the first article; and] that no state, without its consent, shall be deprived of its equal suffrage in the Senate.

Article VI
National Debts

All debts contracted and engagements entered into, before the adoption of this Constitution, shall be as valid against the United States under this Constitution, as under the Confederation.

Supremacy of the National Government

This Constitution, and the laws of the United States which shall be made in pursuance thereof; and all treaties made, or which shall be made, under the authority of the United States, shall be the supreme law of the land; and the judges in every state shall be bound thereby, anything in the constitution or laws of any State to the contrary notwithstanding.

The senators and representatives before mentioned, and the members of the several state legislatures, and all executive and judicial officers, both of the United States and of the several states, shall be bound by oath or affirmation, to support this Constitution; but no religious test shall ever be required as a qualification to any office or public trust under the United States.

Article VII
Ratifying the Constitution

The ratification of the conventions of nine states, shall be sufficient for the establishment of this Constitution between the states so ratifying the same.

Done in convention by the unanimous consent of the states present the seventeenth day of September in the year of our Lord one thousand seven hundred and eighty seven and of the independence of the United States of America the twelfth. In witness whereof we have hereunto subscribed our Names.

Amendment IV

The right of the people to be secure in their persons, houses, papers, and effects, against unreasonable searches and seizures, shall not be violated, and no Warrants shall issue, but upon probable cause, supported by Oath or affirmation, and particularly describing the place to be searched, and the persons or things to be seized.

Report Links

The Internet sites described below can be accessed at http://www.myreportlinks.com

▶**Charters of Freedom: The Bill of Rights**
Editor's Choice Browse primary-source documents from the nation's early days.

▶**CNN: *Cold War***
Editor's Choice Learn about the Cold War, a period marked by intensive spying.

▶**Central Intelligence Agency**
Editor's Choice Take a virtual tour of the CIA, and learn about its operations.

▶**Ben's Guide to U.S. Government for Kids**
Editor's Choice Find out how cases make their way to the Supreme Court and get heard.

▶**Federal Bureau of Investigation**
Editor's Choice Discover the FBI's efforts to fight crime, including its use of high-tech tools.

▶**Landmark Supreme Court Cases: *Mapp v. Ohio* (1961)**
Editor's Choice Learn more about the case that changed the way police gathered evidence.

▶**American Bar Association: Domestic Surveillance**
Find out the American Bar Association's stance on domestic surveillance.

▶**American Civil Liberties Union: Privacy & Technology**
Find out about the ACLU's efforts to maintain Americans' rights to privacy.

▶**Center for Democracy and Technology**
Learn about the Center for Democracy and Technology's efforts to protect free expression and privacy.

▶**Charters of Freedom: High-Resolution Downloads**
Download high-res images of the founding documents of the United States.

▶**Cointel.org**
Read about the federal government's historical efforts to neutralize political dissidents.

▶**Cornell Law School: CRS Annotated Constitution**
Learn about the provisions of the Fourth Amendment.

▶**Electronic Frontier Foundation**
An online discussion of how free speech, privacy, and consumer rights work in the digital age.

▶**Electronic Privacy Information Center (EPIC)**
Find out how privacy issues are playing out in the present day.

▶**Electronic Privacy Information Center: The USA Patriot Act**
Learn the perspective of a group opposed to the USA Patriot Act.

Report Links

The Internet sites described below can be accessed at
http://www.myreportlinks.com

▶**Foreign Intelligence Surveillance Act**
Get a firsthand look at discussions of FISA.

▶**The Founders' Constitution: Amendment IV**
View the political writings that influenced the development of the Fourth Amendment.

▶**How GPS Receivers Work**
Learn how the Global Positioning Systems helps provide people's exact locations.

▶**How Wiretapping Works**
See how easy it is for authorities to tap a telephone line.

▶**Intelligence Activities and the Rights of Americans**
Read the notes of the Church Committee covering domestic spying.

▶**Interactive Constitution: Amendment IV**
This Web site contains the text of the fourth amendment and explains what it means.

▶**National Security Agency**
Learn how the National Security Agency protects the United States and its allies.

▶**Privacy.org, the Site for News, Information, and Action**
Find out about the importance of privacy rights to different groups worldwide.

▶**Privacy Rights Clearinghouse**
See how individuals can maintain their privacy from governments and business.

▶**"The Right to Privacy" by Samuel Warren and Louis D. Brandeis**
Read an early article important in the development of the right to privacy.

▶**The Supreme Court Historical Society**
Get to know more about the history of the U.S. Supreme Court, and how it operates.

▶**Surveillance News Portal**
Learn about the products and techniques used by professionals in the surveillance industry.

▶**U.S. Constitution: Fourth Amendment**
Study the Fourth Amendment and related court cases.

▶**The White House: James Madison**
Learn about the man who pulled together the ideas that went into the Bill of Rights.

▶**The White House: USA PATRIOT Act**
See why President Bush was a strong proponent of the USA Patriot Act.

abolish—Put an end to. Get rid of completely.

affirmation—Statement that is made with complete confidence.

appeal—Request for a higher court to hear and decide on a legal case.

arbitrary—Unreasonable or random.

convicted—Someone who has been convicted of a crime has been found and proven guilty.

Customs Official—Law enforcement officer who checks all goods and people coming in and going out of the country. A Customs Official does not need a warrant or probable cause to search people or vehicles at the border.

eavesdrop—To listen in on a conversation without anyone knowing. An eavesdropper is someone who snoops around.

Exclusionary Rule—Rule that states that any evidence obtained illegally cannot be used in a trial. The rule was intended to make sure that police did not abuse the Fourth Amendment.

Federal Omnibus Crime Control Act—Congress passed this law in 1968. The act gave police the authority to use electronic wiretaps without a warrant if one of the people involved in the conversation gave permission to be listened to and recorded.

harboring—Providing someone or something with shelter and protection.

incorporated—United into one body of law.

intelligence—Information that is gathered and studied about an enemy or potential threat. This information may provide data about a foreign government, their military, corporations, or individuals.

oath—When a person takes an oath, he or she promises to tell the complete truth and nothing but that truth.

roving—Moving or wandering about without direction or purpose.

standards—Rules that are set up and used as examples to follow.

tar and feather—An old fashioned form of punishment and humiliation in which a person would be dipped in tar and then covered with feathers. Usually, this would be done in front of a group of bystanders.

upheld—Supported. Example: "The judge upheld the guilty verdict and the man was sentenced to twenty years in years."

warrant—Legal document issued by a court that gives the authorities permission to do something such as search the home of a citizen.

Chapter 1. The Right to Privacy

1. Book III, Final Report of the Select Committee to Study Governmental Operations With Respect to Intelligence Activities, United States Senate, "Dr. Martin Luther King, Jr., Case Study," *Supplementary Detailed Staff Reports on Intelligence Activities and the Rights of Americans,* April 23, 1976, <www.icdc.com/~paulwolf /cointelpro/churchfinalreportIIIb.htm> (November 2, 2006).

2. Ibid.

3. Ibid.

4. Ibid.

5. Ibid.

6. Book II, Final Report of the Select Committee To Study Governmental Operations With Respect to Intelligence Activities, United States Senate, "B. The Overbreadth of Domestic Intelligence Activity," *Intelligence Activities and the Rights of Americans,* April 26, 1976, <www.icdc.com/~paulwolf/cointelpro/ churchfinalreportIIcb.htm> (November 2, 2006).

7. Ibid.

Chapter 2. The History of the Fourth Amendment

1. Lee Epstein and Thomas G. Walker, *Constitutional Law For a Changing America* (Washington, D.C.: CQ Press, 2001), p. 486.

2. Roger K. Newman, ed., *The Constitution and Its Amendments, Volume 3* (USA: Macmillan Reference, 1999), p. 72.

Chapter 3. The Meaning of the Fourth Amendment

1. Roger K. Newman, ed., *The Constitution and Its Amendments, Volume 3* (USA: Macmillan Reference, 1999), p. 77.

Chapter 4. The Fourth Amendment in Court, 1800–1968

1. U.S. Supreme Court, "Olmstead v. U.S., 277 U.S. 438 (1928)," *FindLaw, Cases and Codes,* n.d., <http://caselaw.lp.findlaw.com/cgibin/getcase.pl?court=us&vol=277&invol=438> (November 2, 2006).

2. Supreme Court Collection, "Brinegar v. United States, 388 U.S. 160 (1949)," *Cornell Law School,* n.d., <www.law.cornell.edu/supct/html/historics/USSC_CR_0338_0160_ZO.html> (November 2, 2006).

3. U.S. Supreme Court, "Mapp v. Ohio, 367 U.S. 643 (1961)," *FindLaw, Cases and Codes,* n.d., <http://caselaw.lp.findlaw.com/scripts/printer_friendly.pl?page=us/367/643.html> (November 2, 2006).

4. Ibid.

5. U.S. Supreme Court, "Aguilar v. Texas, 378

U.S. 108 (1964)," *FindLaw, Cases and Codes,* n.d., <http://caselaw.lp.findlaw.com/scripts/printer_friendly.pl?page=us/378/108.html> (November 2, 2006).

6. Supreme Court of the United States, "389 U.S. 347, 88 S.Ct. 507 (1967)," *Katz v. United States,* n.d., <http://www.soc.umn.edu/~samaha/cases/katz_v_us.html> (November 2, 2006).

7. Ibid.

8. U.S. Supreme Court, "Terry v. Ohio, 392 U.S. 1 (1968)," *FindLaw, Cases and Codes,* n.d., <http://caselaw.lp.findlaw.com/scripts/printer_friendly.pl?page=us/392/1.html> (November 2, 2006).

Chapter 5. The Fourth Amendment in Court, 1969–2000

1. U.S. Supreme Court, "Chimel v. California, 395 U.S. 752 (1969), *FindLaw, Cases and Codes,* n.d., <http://caselaw.lp.findlaw.com/scripts/printer_friendly.pl?page=us/395/752.html> (November 2, 2006).

2. Jimmy Carter, "Foreign Intelligence Surveillance Act of 1978 Statement on Signing S.1566 Into Law," October 25, 1978, *The American Presidency Project,* n.d., <http://www.presidency.ucsb.edu/ws/index.php?pid=30048&st=&st1=> (November 2, 2006).

3. U.S. Supreme Court, "Vernonia School

Dist.47J v. Acton, __U.S. ___ (1995)," *FindLaw, Cases and Codes,* n.d., <http://caselaw.lp.findlaw.com/scripts/printer_friendly.pl?page=us/000/u10263.html> (November 2, 2006).

Chapter 6. The Fourth Amendment Today

1. "The USA PATRIOT Act," *Electronic Privacy Information Center,* November 17, 2005, <http://www.epic.org/privacy/terrorism/usapatriot/> (November 2, 2006).

2. "Bush Defends NSA Spying Program," *CNN.com,* January 1, 2006, <www.cnn.com/2006/POLITICS/01/01/nsa.spying/> November 2, 2006).

3. 107th Congress, "Authorization for Use of Military Force, Public Law 107-40 [S. J. RES. 23]," *FindLaw, Legal News and Community,* September 18, 2001, <http://news.findlaw.com/wp/docs/terrorism/sjres23.es.html> November 2, 2006).

4. "Prepared Remarks for Attorney General Alberto R. Gonzales at the Georgetown University Law Center," *United States Department of Justice,* January 24, 2006, <www.usdoj.gov/ag/speeches/2006/ag_speech_0601241.html> (November 2, 2006).

5. "ABA Resolution 302, Adopted by the House of Delegates," *American Bar Association,* February 13, 2006, <www.abanet.org/op/greco/memos/aba_house302-0206.pdf> (November 2, 2006).

6. George W. Bush, "The President's News Conference," *The American Presidency Project*, January 26, 2006, <http://www.presidency .ucsb.edu/ws/index.php?pid=65146&st=FISA& st1=> (November 2, 2006).

7. CBS/AP, "White House Wants NSA Lawsuits Nixed," *CBS News*, May 27, 2006, <www.cbsnews.com/stories/2006/05/27/ politics/main1662817.shtml> (November 2, 2006).

Freedman, Russell. *In Defense of Liberty: the Story of America's Bill of Rights.* New York: Holiday House, 2003.

Gold, Susan Dudley. *Vernonia School District v. Acton: Drug Testing in Schools.* Tarrytown, N.Y.: Marshall Cavendish Benchmark Books, 2006.

Hossell, Karen Price. *The Bill of Rights.* Chicago, Ill.: Heinemann Library, 2004.

Jacobs, Thomas A. *Young People who Challenged the Law—and Changed Your Life.* Minneapolis, Minn.: Free Spirit Pub., 2006.

Johnson, Terry. *Legal Rights.* New York: Facts On File, 2005.

Kent, Zachary. *James Madison: Creating a Nation.* Berkeley Heights, N.J.: Enslow Publishers, 2004.

Maestro, Betsey. *Liberty or Death: The American Revolution, 1763–1783.* New York: HarperCollins, 2005.

Patrick, John J. *The Supreme Court of the United States: A Student Companion.* New York: Oxford University Press, 2001.

Ramen, Fred. *The Right to Freedom from Searches.* New York: Rosen Pub. Group, 2001.

Seidman, David. *Civil Rights.* New York: Rosen Pub. Group, 2001.

Winters, Robert, ed. *Freedom From Unfair Searches and Seizures.* San Diego, Calif.: Greenhaven Press, 2006.